ROY'S ROT

ILLUSTRATED

ROY'S ROT

Rules of Thumb
To Wit & Wisdom

Roy T. Maloney

DROPZONE
PRESS
P.O. Box 882222
San Francisco
California • 94188

International Standard Book Number: 0-913257-01-X
Copyright © 1985 by Roy T. Maloney
COPYRIGHT © 1980 PORTIONS REPRINTED FROM "REAL ESTATE QUICK & EASY"

Manufactured in the United States of America
Printed by Delta Lithograph Co., Van Nuys, CA
Published by Dropzone Press

Distributed by Publishers Group West, 5855 Beaudry St., Emeryville, CA 94608
Phone: (415) 658-3453

Library of Congress Cataloging in Publication Data:

Maloney, Roy T.
    Roy's Rot

    1. Real estate investment--Quotations, maxims, etc.
2. Real Estate investment--Anecdotes, facetiae, satire,
etc. I. Title.
HD1382.5.M27 1985   332.63'24   85-7015
ISBN 0-913257-01-X (pbk.)

Computer-Composed by T. J. King
Franciscan Systems & Graphics, San Francisco

FIRST PRINTING   JULY, 1985

READ,
THINK,
& THEN WE'LL
TALK . . .

COMPLIMENTS

For their help
with this book
I would like
to thank:
Shakespeare,
Emerson, Goethe,
Cervantes, Aesop,
Confucius, Aristotle,
Einstein, Lincoln,
Tennyson, Montaigne,
and several hundred
others.

The Compiler

CONTENTS

Preface

No one wants to deal with a smart crook,
or a dumb honest person. . . Almost all of us prefer
a knowledgeable person of integrity.

This book represents a few of the shibboleths learned
in twenty-five years of investing. For myself, I cannot separate
dealing with people . . . life . . . and investing.

If the words that follow shed a small ray of light on a formerly
dark area . . . then the purpose has been served.

~ Roy T. Maloney

ILLUSTRATIONS

LISTED IN CHRONOLOGICAL ORDER

QUOTATIONS
FROM
GREAT
LEADERS

Alphabetical by Author

Real estate men sell civilization as much as land.
R.B. Armstrong (economist and author)

Buy on the fringe and wait. Buy land near a growing city! Buy real estate when other people want to sell. Hold what you buy!
John Jacob Astor (1763-1848)

I have always felt that the best security of civilization is the dwelling, and upon properly appointed and becoming dwellings depends more than anything else the improvement of mankind. Such dwellings are the nursery of all domestic virtues.
Benjamin Disraeli, Earl of Beaconsfield (1804-1881)

Land is part of God's estate in the globe: and when a parcel of ground is deeded to you, and you walk over it, and call it your own, it seems as if you had come into partnership with the original proprietor of the earth.
Henry Ward Beecher (1813-1887)

To see the world in a grain of sand,
Infinity in a wild flower,
To hold the earth in the palm of your hand,
And eternity in an hour.
William Blake (1757-1827)

When you own a piece of the earth, you own something Permanent, Real — something that cannot be taken away from you, something that, if intelligently chosen, will provide for your old age.
Arthur Brisbane (1864-1936)

Statisticians advise us to buy stock, but I advise you to buy real estate. When you buy real estate you can go to bed at night perfectly comfortable, for you know it will be there tomorrow. Investments in stocks and bonds, depending as they do largely on management, may be good today and lost tomorrow. A minority stock holder has very little say so as to how his dollar is used. In buying real estate, however, you are the sole owner and manager. You have a freedom of possession which other instruments do not give. No one can freeze you out. No one can run you off. It is yours. I made a real estate deal sixteen years ago against a banker's advice, and sold the property in five years for over $100,000 profit, plus six per cent income. If I had put this profit back in stock, I would have lost practically all of it when the crash came.
Senator W. E. Brock

A fool and his money are soon parted.
George Buchanan (1506-1582)

We recognize the risks of unconventional investing, but the true test of performance in the handling of money is the record of achievement, not the opinion of the respectable. We have the preliminary impression that over the long run caution has cost our colleges and universities much more than imprudence or excessive risk-taking.

McGeorge Bundy, Ford Foundation

All that is necessary for the forces of evil to win the world is for enough good men to do nothing.

Edmund Burke (1729-1797)

Ninety per cent of all millionaires become so through owning real estate. More money has been made in real estate than in all industrial investments combined. The wise young man or wage earner of today invests his money in real estate.

Andrew Carnegie (1837-1919)

Home is the summary of all other institutions.

Chopin (1810-1849)

Land monopoly is not the only monopoly, but it is by far the greatest of monopolies - it is a perpetual monopoly, and it is the mother of all other forms of monopoly.

Winston Churchill (1874-1965)

A man's dignity may be enhanced by the house he lives in.

Cicero (106-43 B.C.)

No investment on earth is so safe, so sure, so certain to enrich its owner as undeveloped realty. I always advise my friends to place their savings in realty near some growing city. There is no such savings bank anywhere.

Grover Cleveland (1837-1908)

The ownership of a home, the feeling of independence that comes with the posession of a bit of the earth are among the most powerful incentives to high civic interest and usefulness.

Calvin Coolidge (1872-1933)

If I could live my life again I would marry early - before twenty years . . . I would have an individual home, no matter where I had to move to get it. I would sacrifice everything . . . to give my bride a spot all her own. As for happiness, I would look for it not in any lasting physical allurement but in our partnership in helping our home and our children grow. For a home must grow too, with the care and love of years until it becomes a part of life - an old friend to whom we willingly return!

Will Durant (in an editorial entitled "Modern Marriage")

Imagination is more important than knowledge
Albert Einstein (1879-1955)

The first farmer was the first man, and all historic nobility rests on possession and use of the land.
Ralph Waldo Emmerson (1803-1882)

Fortune favors the audacious.
Erasmus (1466-1536)

Buying real estate is not only the best way, the quickest way, the safest way, but the only way to become wealthy.
Marshall Field (1835-1906)

Our stock of everything useful, which cannot be increased, becomes more and more valuable because there are more and more people to bid for it. The best example is real estate.
B. C. Forbes (business analyst)

The ownership of an urban home, or a farm, unharassed by fear of loss either through economic pressure or political philosophy, is one of the most stabilizing factors we can have in American civilization.
Glen Frank (noted educator)

If you would know the value of money, go and try to borrow some.

Benjamin Franklin (1706-1790; Poor Richard's Almanac)

No form of property gives as much consequence to its owners as land. This is true of the past, the present, and the future.

James Anthony Froude (1818-1894; historian, in his great work on Caesar)

So far as we can see with any certainty, the quality of value has longer and more consistantly attached to the ownership of land than to any other valuable thing. Everywhere, in all time, among all peoples, the possession of land is the basis of aristocracy, the foundation of great fortunes, the source of power. Those who own the land must be the masters of the rest. Land can exist without labor but labor cannot exist without the land.

Henry George (1839-1897)

Three things are to be looked to in a building: that it stands on the right spot; that it be securely founded; that it be successfully executed.

Goethe (1749-1822)

Wisdom is only found in truth.

(ibid)

Real estate is an imperishable asset, ever increasing in value. It is the most solid security that human ingenuity has devised. It is the collateral to be preferred above all others, and the safest means of investing money.

Hetty Green (One of the world's richest women, 1835-1916)

Believing that nothing can do more toward the development of the highest attributes of good citizenship than the ownership by every family of its own home. I am always glad to endorse effective efforts to encourage home ownership. Nothing better could happen to the United States than a very notable increase in the ownership of homes.

Warren G. Harding (1865-1923)

Land increases more rapidly in value at the centers and about the circumference of cities.

William E. Harmon (noted realty operator)

The present large proportion of families that own their homes is both the foundation of a sound economic and social system and a guarantee that our society will continue to develop rationally as changing conditions demand. A family that owns its own home takes pride in it, maintains it better, gets more pleasure out of it, and has a more wholesome, healthful and happy atmosphere in which to bring up children. The home owner has a constructive aim in life. He works harder outside his home; he spends leisure time more profitably, and he and his family live a finer life and enjoy more of the comforts and cultivating influences of our modern civilization. A husband and wife who own their own home are more apt to save. They have an interest in the advancement of a social system that permits the individual to store up the fruits of his labor. As direct taxpayers they take a more active part in local government. Above all, the love of home is one of the finest instincts and the greatest of inspirations to our people.

Herbert Hoover (1874-1964)

The instinct of ownership is fundamental in man's nature.

William James (1842-1910)

The small landholders are the most precious part of a state.

Thomas Jefferson (1743-1826; Letter 1785)

To be happy at home is the ultimate result of all ambition, the end to which every enterprise and labor tends and of which every desire prompts the prosecution.

Dr. Samuel Johnson (1700-1784)

I have always liked real estate - farm land, pasture land, timber land and city property. I have had experience with all of them. I guess I just naturally like "the good earth," the foundation of all our wealth.

Jesse H. Jones (former federal government financier)

Every man has by nature the right to possess property as his own.

Pope Leo XIII (1810-1903; Encyclical Letter 1891)

Property is the fruit of labor; property is desirable; it is a positive good in the world. That some should be rich shows that others may become rich, and hence is just encouragement to industry and enterprise.

Let not him who is houseless pull down the house of another, but let him work diligently and build one for himself, thus by example assuring that his own shall be safe from violence when built.
Abraham Lincoln (1809-1865)

Property is the only dependable foundation of personal liberty.
Walter Lippmann (1889-1974)

Delay is ever fatal to those who are prepared.
Lucan (A.D. 39-65)

Landlords grow rich in their sleep.
John Stuart Mill (1806-1873)

A man's true wealth is the good he does in the world.
—Mohammed (circa 570-632)

There are so many elements of respectability that come to him who finds permanent shelter for his loved ones. It is a force for law, since a home owner desires protection by law. He wants good, sound government and desires to become an advocate of law and order. Ownership makes him vigilant. I think it was Gladstone who said: "Property always sleeps with one eye open."
John H. Puelicher (president of the American Banker's Association)

Buy land, they ain't making any more of the stuff.
Will Rogers (1879-1935)

Real estate cannot be lost or stolen, nor can it be carried away. Purchased with common sense, paid for in full, and managed with reasonable care, it is about the safest investment in the world.
Franklin D. Roosevelt (1882-1945)

Every person who invests in well-selected real estate in a growing section of a prosperous community adopts the surest and safest method of becoming independent, for real estate is the basis of wealth.
Theodore Roosevelt (1858-1919)

The substantial wealth of man consists in the earth he cultivates, with its pleasant or serviceable animals and plants and the rightly produced work of his own hands.

John Ruskin (1819-1900)

Real estate is an imperishable asset, ever increasing in value. It is the most solid security that human ingenuity has devised. It is the basis of all security, and about the only indestructable security.

Russell Sage (1816-1906)

Land is a fund of a more stable and permanent nature; and the rent of public lands, accordingly, has been the principal source of the public revenue of many a great nation that was much advanced beyond the shepherd state.

The purchase and improvement of uncultivated land is the most profitable employment of the smallest as well as the greatest capitals, and the road to all the fortune which can be acquired in that country "America."

Adam Smith (1723-1790; economist)

The renter who sings "Home Sweet Home" is kidding himself and serenading the landlord. Rent money once handed over is gone forever but the money you put into a house is still yours. It changes its form - it becomes property instead of gold and simply passes from your right pocket to your left.
Billy Sunday (1863-1935; Evangelist)

It is a comfortable feeling to know that you stand on your own ground. Land is about the only thing that can't fly away.
Anthony Trollope (1815-1882)

No matter where you live - in city, village or farm - hang on to your real estate. It's a good investment and worth all that was paid. Real estate at today's prices is the best investment of which I know. Good real estate at the right prices - is sure to be a thrifty investment. People who own real estate should make every effort to keep it. It's worth every dollar it cost.
Thomas Robinson Ward (banker)

Strongly I am impressed with the beneficial effects which our country would receive if every good citizen of the United States owned his own home!
George Washington (1732-1799)

No house should ever be on any hill or on anything. It should be of the hill, belonging to it, so hill and house could live together each the happier for the other.
Frank Lloyd Wright (1869-1959; "An Autobiography," 1932)

ROY'S ROT

Rules of Thumb To Wit & Wisdom

Overview

These bons mots come from widely divergent sources.
They are presented as much for enjoyment value as content, but as the old
Armenian saying goes, "Many a truth was spoken in jest."

1   You can have appreciation of equity without inflation.

2   A poor reason to buy real estate is only for inflation.

3   Inflation should be an added benefit of ownership, not the main reason to purchase.

4   The cost of money, with high interest, can be too high in relation to the benefits.

5   Don't force it, use a bigger hammer.

6   When the cost of money is too high, it can discourage initiative, and in effect act as a hidden tax on the populace.

7   How do you develop a Rodeo Drive (Beverly Hills) with two-year leases? You don't, but rather pipe rack merchandising with hand-written paper signs.

8   The landlord who does not develop longer leases to encourage the development of successful business operations is damaging his own self-interest.

9   A ten-year lease has a "value add" that is more than nine years over a one-year lease.

10   A capitalization rate using a fixed expense factor or percentage, say 40%, that does not account for the exact actual expenses . . . amounts to the same as an inflexible gross rent multiplier.

11   Good news, bad news. The good news is that our five million dollar offer was accepted. The bad news is that they want five hundred dollars down.

12   Main concerns of rental property owners are: rent, vacancies, negative cash flow, maintenance and management.

13 About 80% of the population cannot afford to purchase a home. Equity participation is one answer.

14 I can show you how to build a clock, but you will have to wind it.

15 Fake it 'til you make it.

16 I've been down so long it feels like up.

17 What goes around, comes around.

18 The feeling that you understand real estate is similar to being able to hit a speed punching bag at five beats per second while blindfolded.

19 On any particular job it takes about two weeks to learn the rules, and a lifetime to learn the exceptions.

20 There are as many definititions of net, or profit, as there are people.

21 Why do you spend so much time arguing over a contract when you have no intention of living up to it? To provide a basis for renegotiation.

22 It is difficult, if not impossible, to prepare an economic model when this model can be influenced by political decisions.

23 The greatest potentiating effect in real estate is to buy property with nothing or low down payment. Then sell at a profit. Or to create an increase in rental income with a disproportionate increase in fair market value, which represents an increase in equity.

24 After you have established a solid base of income property with a positive cash flow... and then lose it on a misadventure, you won't miss it anymore than you would your eyes.

25 Nothing is more dangerous than an idea when it is the only one you have. —*Emile Chartier*

HOMER
Greek poet
8th century B.C.

26 A simple handwritten statement of facts on an agreement that is witnessed and notarized is a very powerful tool in a court of law. Remember that with a contract handwritten text takes precedence over typewritten, and typewritten takes precedence over the pre-printed form.

27 The way to succeed is to double your failure rate.
—*Thomas J. Watson, founder of IBM*

28 A rich man with a problem is mother's milk for an attorney.

29 A friend in Alaska states that turnkey (completed) construction by a contractor costs about $80 per square foot, including land. The same quality of manufactured housing made in the "lower 48" and shipped to Alaska runs turnkey about $50 a square foot. The difference being in the increased cost of labor and material in Alaska.

30 A capitalization rate fanatic using a percentage rate of expense that he found in an erudite statistical manual that will not vary based on the actual expenses... is like a statistician who averages the temperature of your body, even though one foot is on ice and the other on fire.

31 I have two buildings for you both priced the same... one has a cap rate of 10%, the other 11%... which one do you want? Only a fool would purchase on these facts alone.

32 The problem with a real IRR (Internal Rate of Return), or FMRR, is that there is none until after the fact.

33 On a foreclosure sale, and others, it is a good idea to come prepared for an overbid with ten or more $5,000 cashier's checks. You will be way ahead of the person who has not thought it through.

34 If you plug in too many variables into a projection, e.g. IRR (Internal Rate of Return)... the computer printout is not worth the paper it is printed on.

35 An interesting viewpoint: On a 100% financed purchase money mortgage, all of the seller's equity is the buyer's debt.

36 Time is money . . . don't waste it.

37 One difference between an amateur and a professional is the assumption by the professional of a positive outcome.

38 Both Michaelangelo and Le Corbusier observed that the height reached by their upstreched arm was two times the height from the ground to their navel. They also observed that their navel height compared to their full height was in the ratio of 1 to 1.6. The proportions of the golden section. It is interesting to note that two belly buttons were the inspiration for so much beauty.

39 This book has taken me from local obscurity to national oblivion.

40 The three circles in Chinese architecture and design represent: science, beauty and religion.

41 Beauty, charm, intelligence, health and wealth. . . help, but aren't everything. There is a strong relationship between knowledge, power, ability, excellence, happiness and the creation of wealth.
   The ability to use knowledge is power. The ability to use this power, within the limits of your own capability in the pursuit of excellence, creates happiness and wealth.
   There are many men with the knowledge of football equal to Vince Lombardi, but few apply this knowledge in the pursuit of excellence as he did. This outlook is the thread through the lives of men like Lincoln, Patton, Frank Lloyd Wright and Zeckendorf.

42 Better to have a real estate loan with limited liability than a personal loan with unlimited liability.

43 Worst case with a real estate loan, lender takes property . . . with a personal loan, lender takes you.

44 There has been more money lost in real estate through over optimism than through over pessimism.

45 If you can't do the time, don't do the crime.

46 Lack of opportunity is usually nothing more than lack of purpose and direction.

47 Bankruptcy is the financial equivalent of making a man a eunuch.

48 On the front door of your property place a sign that reads: In emergency phone ... Number of children ... Number of pets ... Type of pets ... Special medical information ... For ...

49 Tough times don't last, tough people do.

50 If, as the ads claim all you need is knowledge of real estate to make your fortune ... why aren't all the real estate agents and brokers who have this information millionaires?

51 Nothing down, wonderful. Negative cash flow, not good. Fast fuse balloon payment, bad. No financing to be had, very bad. Foreclosure imminent, disaster.

52 Go for Cash. When you must take paper ... increase the note by an amount indicated on the "present value of the dollar" table. If this is not clear then review "Internal Rate of Return" and "Discounted Cash Values."

53 The one who loves the least has the power.

54 I thought I was wrong, but I was mistaken.

55 Before granting a loan, a banker likes to know: Will you pay? Can you pay, and did you pay?

56 Babe Ruth led the league in strike outs the year he led in home runs.

57 Jealous people revel in drawing attention to other people's failures.

SOCRATES
Greek philosopher
c. 470 B.C. - 399 B.C.

58 Living well is the best revenge.

59 Fool me once, shame on you. Fool me twice, shame on me.

60 A bird in the hand ... means it's difficult to blow your nose.

61 Fixed and non-fixed loans ... quick and easy: With a fixed loan the interest and loan payments do not change for the life of the loan. With a non-fixed loan (or mortgage) the interest rate can change with the CPI, treasury bill rate or other interest rate indicator. When the interest rate changes, so therefore does the loan payment and/or the length of the loan.

62 It is rare, if ever, when *all* aspects of real estate are down. If housing sales are down ... rental sales increase. If residential income is down ... commercial sales can be doing well. Know your market.

63 When you are reclined on your cantilevered sundeck overlooking the crashing surf and sipping your pina colada ... it is hard to feel like a loser. You can create your own ambience for success.

64 When you are considering the purchase of two similar properties, one of which is in poor repair, but much less expensive... obtain firm quotes to have this property equal or exceed the quality of the other property. If the total cost of the property including remodeling is less than the cost of the improved property ... then your choice becomes obvious. Fortunes are made creating beauty out of nothingness.

65 When you are calculating your potential profits on a transaction ... remember to include the cost of carrying a loan. A million dollar loan at 20% is $200,000 for the year. This can eat you alive.

66 People can be divided into three groups: those who *make* things happen, those who *watch* things happen, and those who *wonder* what happened.

67 The road to success is always under construction.

68 If your goal is to have one hundred million dollars ... invest one million today at ten per cent interest and wait 48 years.

69 Greed for land is unknown to the Australian aborigines. When they grasp a handful of earth and let it sift through their fingers, it is not to covet the earth, but to enhance their feeling of being as one with the universe.

70 It seems logical that the cost of a lease should be at least as much as the interest the owner could receive at the bank on the fair market value of the property.

71 If you buy property to own and not to sell ... then you won't be sorry if you must hold for a distant sale.

72 The wine is more important than the bottle. The use of real estate can be more important than the property.

73 If you are the owner of two buildings consider connecting them with an arched skylight. This "streetscape," an open-ended pedestrian thoroughfare, would do well to emulate the Gallerias of Milan and San Francisco.

74 Too many people are busy being busy.

75 Leveree, the one who is being leveraged.

76 The investor in an equity participation deal wants to leverage his investment about 2½ times. For example, 20% down payment to return 50% on the profit.

77 You have two diverse philosophies at work with rental property. The landlord is trying to make a living on his investment. The tenant is not concerned if the property makes money, he wants a nice place to live. These different objectives are the basis of most tenant problems. Common objectives will help solve the problem.

78 A broker on the rocks has his license on ice.

79 One point on a million dollars is $10,000 or 1%.

80 A seller who does not want to have the problems of management, but does want the benefit of appreciation on the property, should consider an equity participation plan. The seller can leave cash (equity) in for the down payment portion of his participation, say 20% for 50% of the profit (over the new purchase price) in five years. The buyer has the advantage of buying for little or nothing down. The seller can have his cake and eat it too.

81 When you have a split of spouses from a home ... you have an in-house spouse and an out-house spouse.

82 Advertising costs, publicity is free.

83 Two rules of success: First, innoculate yourself with the worst possible scenario ... you will then develop antibodies against failure. Second, visualize the goals you wish to obtain. When you are there it will be *deja vu*.

84 *Using the "rule of 72," a property worth $200,000 and increasing in value, based on an inflation rate of 8% per year, will be worth $400,000 in 9 years. Wait another 9 years and it will be worth $800,000. Patience is definitely a virtue.*

84 *If your tenant is late with the rent, any late fees can be subtracted from the security deposit.*

85 *One standard with equity sharing is that the tenant in common who is the investor and puts up 20% of the purchase price as down payment, will receive 50% of the tax write-offs and 50% of the profit on sale of the property in five years.*

86 *Negative leverage, or reverse leverage, occurs when debt service is larger than the net income. There is a negative cash flow.*

87 *Negative amortization occurs when the loan payments are not high enough to pay all of the interest. The loan principal is therefore becoming larger, rather than smaller. Our federal government has this problem.*

88 Beware of reckless eyeballing of hysterical monuments.

89 Take an expert to lunch and you pay. It is the most cost-effective way to obtain information without any phone interruptions.

90 What is scarce today will be scarcer tomorow.

91 80% of all sales are made after the 5th call.
48% of salespeople quit after 1 call.
25% of salespeople quit after 2 calls.
12% quit after 3 calls.
5% quit after 4 calls.
10% keep on calling and then make 80% of all sales.

92 People do what you *in*spect, not what you expect.

93 In lieu of cash you could put in new carpets and drapes as a security deposit.

94 Name a tax write-off received without spending any dollars? Depreciation.

95 ABC... Always Be Closing (the deal).

96 KYMS ... Keep Your Mouth Shut.

97 You have two ears and one mouth... and they should be used in about that proportion.

98 KISS ... Keep It Simple, Stupid.

99 We have two choices... to be an axe or a chopping block. The neck on the block belongs to the one who does not choose.

100 One day you are drinking wine, the next day picking the grapes.

101 Better to have a 50% tax on $20,000 and keep $10,000 tax-free, than a $10,000 loss (write-off) and keep nothing. Note that the difference between the two examples is $20,000. Don't outsmart yourself with tax losses.

102 So you do not want the extra $100,000 in cash now on the sale of your property because it will put you in a higher tax bracket. Wait a minute and analyze. You will pay tax on the $100,000 when you finally do receive it. Could you not pay the tax, invest the $100,000 and make enough on the investment to pay any additional tax?

103 It's hard by the yard, but a cinch by the inch.

104 As the urban cowboy was "looking for love in all the wrong places," so the investor can with real estate.

105 Out of the mud grows the lotus.

106 Jesus saves, but Moses invests.

107 On a foreclosure property, or REO (Real Estate Owned property), it is prudent to be on good terms with the bank or savings and loan manager who lists these properties as he can give you special insight.

108 Edifice complex: a mania to build.

109 If you have one million dollars going into escrow, then wire funds bank to bank (electronic transfer) without a check, in order for interest to start at the exact close of escrow.

110 When you work on solutions try not to become part of the problem.

111 Make lemonade out of the lemon.

112 Forewarned forearmed. —*Cervantes*

113 Albert Einstein used his Princeton University paychecks as bookmarks.

PLATO
Greek philosopher
c. 428 B.C. - c. 348 B.C.

114 If you are so smart, why aren't you rich?

115 Pitching always comes before hitting.

116 Publish or perish.

117 If it is too good to be true, it probably is.

118 It's not how much smoke you blow, it's how hard you blow it.

119 The most creative financing of the future could well be the limited partnership syndication, including equity participation.

120 Avulsion is fast, erosion is slow.

121 If you are going to play the market, be a bull or a bear ... not a pig.

122 We will sell no house before its time.

123 Nothing down ... balloons up ... get a longer string.

124 The easiest person to deceive is oneself.

125 What "rosebud" was to Citizen Kane, the tattooed words above the wings on the arm of a fellow paratrooper are to me: "Death before Dishonor."

126 You can't tell ... but you can *sell* a book by its cover.

127 Cash is king ... but a well "seasoned" (good record of payment), high interest, and secured note is a prince.

128 You are what you think.

129 Keep your eye on the doughnut, not the hole.

130 Your goals and purpose on this planet should be crystal clear.

131 Technical information doubles every five years. Are you keeping up?

132 Try to find a job you like; don't just look for wealth.

133 Inundata ... too much data.

134 Work *smart* and hard, not just hard.

135 The ring of depressed property around the center of a vibrant growing city is one area of investment opportunity.

136 Make stepping stones out of stumbling blocks.

137 Make it snappy and be unhappy.

138 A penny held over your eye can blot out your vision.

139 Move one grain of sand and you change the entire structure of the universe.

140 All the darkness in the world cannot put out the light of one candle.

141 There is more objection to the tax complications than there is to the amount of the tax. —*Ronald Reagan*

142 If the owner of a commercial property has a problem he usually thinks in terms of selling. A possible better solution is to have a professional management firm take over and create a Master Ground Lease (MGL) with triple net to the owner.

143 Make your move. It is usually easier to apologize than to get permission.

144 A ship in port is safe, but that is not what ships were built for.

145   If you are not familiar with corbellated dentillated soffits, rococo entablatures, and italianate curvilinear broken pediments . . . you are probably not familiar with good architecture. But you can still appreciate it.

146   The harder you work, the luckier you get.

147   You can judge a country by the way it treats its least favored citizen.
—*John F. Kennedy*

148   Truth hurts less than a discovered lie.

149   Color code a floor plan of all exits and place in halls.

150   SET . . . Spendable, Equity and Taxable.

151   I know you think you know what I mean, but I am not sure you realize that what you thought I mean was not what I said.

152   It only takes twenty years for a liberal to become a conservative without changing a single idea.

153   Stalin's paranoia was a self-fulfilling prophecy; so was Bucky Fuller's optimism.

154   In monopoly capitalism, price usually equals at least cost plus taxation plus rent plus interest.

155   Poverty doth make cowards of us all.
—*Joseph Labadie*

156   Every law creates a whole new criminal class overnight.

157   If this is an out-of-the-body experience, I may never have to go out of my mind again.

158   It is not possible to step into the same river twice. —*Heraclitus*

ARISTOTLE
Greek philosopher
384 B.C. - 322 B.C.

159 Don't be a captain steering by the wake.

160 There is nothing so unthinkable as thought, unless it be the entire absence of thought. —*Samuel Butler*

161 WHO DARES WINS. —*Motto of the British SAS.*

162 When a project is in trouble, the investor from Jackass Flats says, "How many days have I left?" The investor from Beverly Hills says, "How much money will it take to cure the problem?"

163 If an investment property breaks even, it is making money because of the tax factors and equity build-up.

164 If you purchase a $60,000 condo for investment and it breaks even... then, worst case, with no inflation for 30 years ... you should have a $60,000 nest egg. If you had five you could probably retire in style.

165 Wealth is something other than money ... as wisdom is something other than knowledge.

166 There is no five-year lease on life renewable at your option.

167 Avoid the "big pot" concept of throwing everything into one project ... have individual profit centers so that you can track performance.

168 If people say "yes" to me fifteen days out of the year, I am a success.

169 Rewards are not automatic.

170 Property management developed as a profession during the great depression ... when banks took over property and were forced to manage them.

171 When done right, both making money and spending it can be enjoyable.

172 To sleep nights and not be concerned with bank or savings and loan "demand for full payment of loan," notify the lender of assumption of any loan, and obtain the lender's approval in writing, before you assume the loan. Or see a real estate attorney to arrange a "special handling."

173 It takes all of our knowledge to make things simple.

174 Same bed, different dream.

175 The only shelter in real estate is depreciation ... taxes, interest and expenses are write-offs. There is a difference between shelter and write-offs. With a shelter, there is no cash out-of-pocket, but with a write-off there *is* cash out-of-pocket.

176 Concerned about losing half or all of a property to a wife or live-in? Then consider having them sign and record a "quit claim deed."

177 On a normal foreclosure sale there is a "trustee's deed." On a probate sale there is an "executor's deed," and on a court decree there is a "decree of distribution," which is like a deed.

178 The quintessential communication for clarity was by a Navy pilot flying over the Atlantic during WWII. He stated, "Sighted sub, sank same."

179 He is only rich who owns the day. —*Ralph Waldo Emerson*

180 Pay long term capital gains, but shelter ordinary income.

181 To be successful and happy, you should be the same person at work that you are at home.

182 The investor has a cash register, the occupant has a home.

183 In real estate you get into trouble not for what you know but for what you *don't* know.

184   Soar like an eagle — go for it.

185   To fully experience the beauty and safety of a sailing ship in a harbor, you must first experience the danger of a turbulent sea.

186   Peel the onion a bit.

187   Considering the alternatives, democracy is the best form of government. —*Winston Churchill*

188   Knowing math does not make an engineer, any more than knowing real estate law makes an investor.

189   To eliminate "cash flow deficiency," raise rentals and lower expenses.

190   Have you noticed that highly mortgaged (leveraged) properties catch fire, and burn, more readily than free and clear property?

191   POEM ... Plan, Organize, Execute, and Manage.

192   Once you have it made (or come close) you will want to consider a "diversified portfolio" for "capital preservation," and to be prepared for the unknown. Such a portfolio would include: cash to cover six months' expenses, stocks, municipal and corporate bonds, money market funds, precious metals, gold and silver coins, gemstones, etc.

193   Remember when an ice cream cone cost only 50¢? Remember when the average house cost only $50,000? Each generation has a different perspective on standard values.

194   Need a million dollar loan? It may well be worth hiring a mortgage banker to help you.

195   An insurance replacement *policy is better than a* depreciated *policy*

196   *The right time to duplicate your keys is before they are lost.*

MARCUS TULLIUS CICERO
Roman author and statesman
January 3, 106 B.C. - December 7, 43 B.C.

197 When a master lease is cancelled the sub-leases are usually automatically also cancelled. Watch your sub-lease.

198 You found the perfect property, but can't swing it. Option the property. Write up a complete prospectus, with profit and loss projections, and include inside and outside photos. Obtain a top syndicator to help you form a partnership. Then purchase with up to five other people as limited partners.

199 Never step back when you can step forward . . . to the side if you must.

200 As per military operations: "Be prepared to hit targets of opportunity."

201 If you can't handle all of the wine, women and song . . . stop singing.

202 I can sometimes do the work of two men. —*Laurel and Hardy.*

203 The poor save and the rich spend. (As told to the author by a loan officer)

204 In almost all cities the Recorder's Office posts Notices of Default on a bulletin board. Looking at these on a regular basis (or by subscribing to a local private service) you might find an excellent property to bid on.

205 Non-veterans can obtain veteran's property and loans by bidding on them in foreclosure.

206 The tax laws written for the Rockefellers and the Vanderbilts also apply to the self-employed.

207 The key to taxes on the self-employed is the net-income, not the gross.

208 You pay taxes all year long, so *think* taxes all year long. Keep a log of expenses.

209 In the past two years at least eight nondescript buildings have been converted to bed and breakfast inns in the San Francisco area. The rentals increasing from about $300 per month, or $10 per day, to $100 per day, a tenfold increase in rental income.

210 For an instant MBA remember three things:
1) Sign all checks yourself until gross sales exceed one hundred million dollars.
2) Never spend money in anticipation of closing a deal.
3) Starting small borrow increasingly large amounts from your banker, but pay it all back punctually. —*Victor Palmieri*

211 The lintel low enough to keep out pomp and pride.
The threshold high enough to turn deceit aside;
The doorband strong enough from robbers to defend.
This door will open at a touch to welcome any friend.
—*Henry Van Dyke*

212 Bottom line on loans: Don't assume you can assume.

213 The grapevine is a goldmine.

214 So the seller wants $200,000 and not a penny less. Fine . . . I will buy it. Here are my terms: Buyer closing costs and real estate agents commission to be used as the total down payment. Real estate agents commission to be in the form of a straight note, due in full in one year, at an interest rate of 12% per annum. Remaining balance to be in the form of a first loan, payable on a monthly basis, based on an amortization rate of 30 years, with no payment for 90 days from close of escrow, and due in full in 15 years. Buyer to have the right of one transfer of the loan with the same terms and conditions, to a person of worthy credit.

215 Upon the sale of your property the chances are excellent that you have pre-paid your insurance for one year, and have a rebate or credit available to you in escrow. Remember the insurance company will not be looking for you with money in hand.

216 Success is never certain, failure is never final.

217 Most title and escrow companies extend a considerable discount on their fees if you buy and sell the same property within two years. Just ask.

218 If you have a property in foreclosure, consider having the holder of the first loan sell it back to you at the foreclosure sale. The price you pay being the balance of the first loan plus all foreclosure costs, and this total amount being in the form of a new first loan. You are gambling that the holders of the secondary financing will not outbid you. If they don't, you have wiped out all secondary financing with the foreclosure sale.

219 If it looks like a duck, quacks like a duck, and walks like a duck ... it's a duck.

220 To cover both a high and a low price for tax purposes you may want to have a clause on your deposit receipt that reads: Price is estimated to have a fair market value of $80,000, but is being sold for $70,000 to help cover any repair expenses.

221 Taking a secret profit and then trying to give it back, is like trying to un-rob a bank. Kickbacks are a form of secret profit. The statute of limitations for secret profit is usually ten years.

222 Dead bodies surface.

223 On a deposit receipt the phrase "Property to be purchased in 'as is' condition" is an illusory phrase and cannot apply to hidden or latent defects that are known by either the seller or the agent and not disclosed to the buyer. The seller can write on a deposit receipt, "to the best of his knowledge" there are no latent or hidden defects, and that it is recommended that the buyer hire a licensed contractor to prepare a full report.

224 Weak case, ask for jury; strong case, ask for judge.

225 In a jury trial, the tenant screens jurors for tenants, the landlord screens jurors for landlords.

226 It's not the principle of the thing, it's the money.

227 Knowledge of agent is knowledge of fiduciary of that agent.

228 An agent must present all offers to the seller, even after another offer is accepted. In that case the agent should tell the seller it can be used as a "back up" offer, and should be careful of "breach of contract" if seller breaches the accepted offer.

229 The agent of the seller has the duty to be "fair and honest" to the buyer, even though there is no fiduciary relationship.

230 Use different colored checks for each property account.

231 Landlord can state on lease, "To be occupied only by humans."

232 When a contractor wants to lower the interest rate on houses that he is selling, he can "buy-down" the interest rate. To lower the interest rate 1% for two years would cost about 2 points (2%). For example: If the actual rate of a loan is 13% and the lender wants to have an interest rate of 10%, the rate can be bought-down for 2 points times 3%, or 6%. The buy-down on a $100,000 loan would therefore be $6,000. After two years the interest would revert back to 13%.

233 A future trend in building is to have two or more identical master bedrooms, with a shared living area and kitchen. The house then lends itself to an easy division for two or more persons.

234 The number of shell houses, that is, houses that you finish yourself, is on the increase.

235 TIP ... Tailored Installment Program, a variable loan usually with lower initial payments and then payment increases.

236 To calculate 6 months' interest, take ½ of the yearly interest. So 16% per annum is equal to 8% for 6 months.

237 To help sell income property guarantee the rents for one year. Also, you can pre-pay the real estate taxes (tax write-off), so that you can advertise no real estate taxes for one or more years.

238 Having trouble selling a property? Consider selling only the building, and leasing the land to the buyer. You can then sell the land lease to someone else, or keep it for the cash flow.

239 Blended rate . . . your old loan is at 10% interest, and you want to increase the principal amount, but you don't want to pay the new higher interest, say 14%. Then negotiate with the lender for a blended rate on the new loan of 12%.

240 Great spirits have always encountered violent opposition from mediocre minds. —*Albert Einstein*

241 Leasing the land under improved property is a form of financing.

242 Watch out for reverse leverage . . . where the leveragor becomes the leveragee.

243 Sometimes the means to an end becomes the end.

244 The disruption in your life of five moves is about equal to one fire.

245 What you think of me is none of my business.

246 The map never equals the territory.

247 Of two explanations, the simpler one is more likely to be correct.

248 Knowing when not to make, is as important as knowing when to make a deal.

249 Be sure to determine who are the buyers and who are the sellers.

250 Be careful of what you dream. You may get it.

PETRARCH (Francesco Petrarca)
Italian poet
July 20, 1304 - July 19, 1374

251 A high interest note that is unsaleable can be wrapped (AIDT) with a lower interest note with a higher principal.
Example: An $80,000 note at 16% interest can be wrapped with a $100,000 loan at 12%.
   Conclusion: Wrap a bad loan with a good loan, and work on the lower interest (a negative wrap), and the increased principal amount.

252 Greater uncertainty, then you need greater liquidity.

253 Vigorish... Mafia interest on a loan has been reported at 5% per week.

254 When the interest rate goes up, the equity goes down.

255 It's difficult to soar with eagles when you work with turkeys.

256 Go duck hunting where the ducks are.

257 What isn't what it is, until it isn't what it is? Answer: Equity.

258 Only a mediocre person is always at his best. —*Somerset Maugham*

259 Equal dignities rule ... have authority in writing even if you have a telegram.

260 Certain government agencies ... Never have so few spent so much for so little.

261 If it was easy, everybody would be doing it.

262 A $100,000 loan with an interest of 11.75% per annum, and fully amortized in 30 years, will have a monthly payment of $1,010 (round number) per month. In 30 years when paid off, you will have paid $363,600! ... Will they take $90,000 cash?

263 Look for opportunity, not guarantees.

264 A billion here, a billion there, and pretty soon you have spent some real money.

265 In earthquake country, consider seismic anchor bolts. A steel bracket is placed on the stud, a bolt is then placed through the bracket, mud sill, and foundation. By securing the mud sill to the foundation, it helps to prevent the house from slipping off its foundation.

266 Need an extra room and can spare about $2,000? Consider the SPADOME of Redondo Beach, CA, a most interesting geodesic dome. It is made of clear Lexan, and one model is 12 feet in diameter by 9 feet high. The design is based on futurist Buckminster Fuller's 1951 patent.

267 My price, your terms; your price, *my* terms.

268 ABC — Abundance of Caution.

269 AITD — All inclusive trust deed (wraparound)

270 A first or second loan could be paid in ounces of gold (as law allows) to protect the lender from inflation. For example, you could have a contract to accept two ounces of gold per month for ten years.

271 An individual who joint ventures with a 'dealer,' may then become a 'co-dealer.'

272 As the twig is bent, so the tree grows.

273 A ten — A scale from one to ten used for buildings and women (or men). There are no tens, but you can have two fives.

274 A visit to or by the IRS is now a part of every businessman's life. If you keep good records you will look forward to an IRS audit the way St Augustine looked forward to confession.

275 Avoid the financial PIT (Probate, Inflation & Taxes).

276 BAR SALE — The seven services of the real estate industry: Buy, Appraise, Rent, Sell, Auction, Lease & Exchange.

277 Battles are won in the tents of generals before the battle begins.

278 Better a $200 attorney's fee than a $20,000 legal error.

279 Better to make a fortune slowly than a bundle quickly.

280 Be your own banker; lend money.

281 Be careful out there. A constructive receipt of money (even 'paper') can ruin your tax plans.

282 Bigger fool theory — It doesn't matter what you pay for a building, there is always a bigger fool to pay more.

283 Bluebird — A semi-professional with the MOFIA.

284 Buy vacation property during the worst weather, and sell during the best.

285 Capital punishment — is when the government taxes you to get capital in order to go into business in competition with you, and then taxes the profits in your business in order to pay for its losses.

286 CCCL — Elements of a contract: Consent, Capacity, Consideration & Lawfulness.

287 Checking credibility — If the borrower doesn't ask about the interest rate, then the lender better.

288 CIGAR — Major sub-markets of real estate: Commercial, Industrial, Governmental, Agricultural & Residential.

289 COC — Cash On Cash.

GEOFFREY CHAUCER
English author
c. 1340 - 1400

290 COLIC — Essentials of a contract: Competent parties, Offer & acceptance, Legality of object, In writing & signed, & Consideration.

291 Concretion as opposed to abstraction.

292 COW — Code Of West (gentlemen's agreement).

293 CRAM — Condominium Reverse Annuity Mortgage.

294 Curtilage — The enclosed ground space around a building, such as lawn or patio.

295 DIC — Doric, Ionic & Corinthian in order of architectural antiquity.

296 Do it once, do it right, and do it now.

297 Don't use a meat cleaver for eye surgery.

298 Don't use your money, use other people's money (OPM).

299 DUE — Disposition, Use, Exclusions, as they relate to ownership.

300 DUST — Essentials of value: Demand, Utility, Scarcity, & Transferability.

301 Economic history teaches us that adversity breeds opportunity.

302 Economies of scale — The more units, the greater the volume discount.

303 Figures don't lie, but liars can figure.

304 GAM — Gross Annual Multiplier (same as GRM — Gross Rent Multiplier).

305 Gather ye rosebuds while ye may.

306 Gift your house to a charitable organization, then take a tax write-off for the value of the house, and live in your gift for the rest of your life.

307 GIGO — Garbage In, Garbage Out.

308 GNOME—ENCLATURE.

309 Golden Rule — Whoever has the gold makes the rules.

310 Go to a stationery store (or title company) and buy a pre-printed *note*. Then type in an amount equal to the equity in your house, and with payment terms that are comfortable. You have now created an instrument that can be used as down payment on any property you desire. Note that no cash has been used, only a piece of paper that represents value.

311 Hemingway buyer — A rich person. When Hemingway was aked how the rich are different, he said, "They have more money."

312 If interest rates rise — all other things being equal — the price of property should fall.

313 If it is not money, it is not a lien. An *encumbrance* is not always a *lien,* but a lien is always an encumbrance.

314 If there are no 'right to light' laws in your city, be sure before you install a solar energy system that you won't be 'overshadowed.'

315 If there is a chance you will not qualify for a loan on a property, have the seller refinance and take out a large portion of his cash in this manner. As a buyer you can then assume the new loan from the seller. It is easier to assume an existing loan than to create a new one.

316 If the seller wants your cash and not paper, use your property as down payment, but 'guarantee the sale of property within 18 months.'

317 If you do not know a city, try a sightseeing bus tour (both the pleasure tour and the business tour). At a minimum you will then know the key areas and not appear to be a real estate dummy.

318 If you work 40 weeks a year (excluding all vacations and holidays), five days a week, or 200 days per year, and make $200,000, you are averaging $1,000 per day. If you make $100,000, it is $500 per day. $50,000 per year is $250 per day, and $25,000 per year is $125 per day. Equity build up could be included as part of the income as it is adding to your net worth. Did you make your quota today?

319 In certain sections of government, they keep the monkeys and cut down the tallest trees.

320 In contracts, the big print giveth and the small print taketh away.

321 In direct relation to the costs of transportation, energy, fuel, land, etc., the move back to the city becomes more practical, and the need to improve the rotting core increases.

322 In the land of the blind, the one-eyed man is king.

323 Invest in inflation. It's the only thing going up.

324 Investors should have the ability to visualize property *after* improvements.

325 It is easier to get in a project than to get out.

326 It is possible and practical under certain circumstances to make a *'two-tier price offer.'* One price under one condition, and an increased price under another condition.

327 It only makes sense to borrow money when the cost of borrowing is less than the return on the invested money.

328 KELVIN MOF — A MOF with no money down. Kelvin refers to the term in physics of "absolute zero."

329 Land has an infinite useful life.

DESIDERIUS ERASMUS
Dutch theologian and scholar
c. 1469 - 1536

330 Land salesmen have a lot on their minds.

331 Land should double in value every five years. This will help cover inflation, taxes and payments.

332 Leverage is the use of borrowed money to magnify gains and losses.

333 Lost opportunity cost. Take the money and run. The dollars you must discount to receive the money now, subtracted from the dollars to be made by having the money now, is the *lost opportunity cost.* So why lose?

334 Margin of Appreciation (MOA) — The difference in interest between the inflation rate and your loan rate, *e.g.,* if inflation is 14% and your loan is 12%, you have a 2% MOA. It can be positive or negative.

335 MOF — Mount Olympus Formula, or modified option formula.

336 MOFIA — Mount Olympus Formula Investment Advisor.

337 Mondo Com Condo — All (100%) commercial condominiums.

338 Much easier to squeeze the toothpaste out of a tube than to put it back.

339 New things succeed, as former things grow old.

340 Next to a bad tenant, a vacancy is a delight.

341 Number of square feet times the cost per square foot (average for area), equals the estimated price of the building or unit.

342 On a lease, set the rent at, say, $500 per month, but if paid on the *first* of the month it is $475.

343 On a tax deferred exchange — Too much equity, then refinance. Too little equity, then pay down the loan.

344 One hand washes the other.

345 One story of a building is about 10 feet high. A ten story building is about 100 feet high.

346 Pay all cash to lower the purchase price, on the order of a 20% discount, then immediately obtain an 80% loan.

347 People who know how, work for people who know *why*.

348 Prepayment penalties for paying off a loan early run about the cost of six month's interest.

349 PSZTUL — (PISTOL): Physical Structure, Zoning, Transportation, Utilities & Land are points to check in the purchase of an industrial site.

350 RAW — Ready, Able & Willing. Referring to buyers in an open market to establish a fair market value.

351 Record options and other contracts to help protect your position against future liens.

352 REDI — Rapport, Empathy, Demeanor & Integrity. The author's guidelines.

353 Regarding tax shelters — Consider paying taxes and keeping a smaller profit. Taxes as yet do not exceed 100%.

354 Return on capital is less in a richer country and more in a poorer country.

355 Reverend Ike might be right, "Money is beautiful," (at least what can be done with it).

356 REX — Real Estate Exchange, a tax-deferred exchange (Section 1031, Federal Tax Code).

357 RIC — Reverse Income Condominium (a turkey).

358 RIP — Reverse Income Property (another loser).

359 RURBAN — Transition area from rural to urban.

360 Since cold water is used the most, check the cold water flow on the top floor when inspecting a building.

361 SIP — Sensible Income Project (a winner).

362 Six 'P' Formula — Poor prior preparation = pretty poor performance.

363 Tenants who lose keys and then break windows and doors to gain entry ... and then ask why the landlord doesn't take care of the place, are a little like the man who killed his mother and father, and then asked for mercy because he was an orphan.

364 The best advice you will ever pay for is professional real estate counseling.

365 The best investment on earth ... is earth.

366 The building is not overpriced, you are under-paid.

367 The buyer who has himself as a real estate agent may have a fool as a client.

368 The cost approach for appraising buildings usually results in the *highest* appraisal. It is practical to use on new buildings, and *one of a kind* buildings, e.g., post office, church, or city hall.

369 The cost of having nothing is going up. Being broke isn't the luxury it used to be. High inflation irrevocably separates the rich from the poor.

370 The essence of good architecture is not only superb design, but also superior economics.

371 The four C's of credit are Capacity, Collateral, Character & Cash.

372 The goal of government should be to provide the opportunity for all citizens to own a home.

373 Throughout recorded history a fine suit cost about one ounce of gold; a superior dwelling, a thousand ounces.

374 'Time spent on reconnaissance is never wasted.' —*A military dictum*

375 The Robie house in Chicago, and "Falling Waters" in Bear Run, Pennsylvania, are probably two of the most architecturally important houses in America.

376 To establish a good credit rating, deposit $1,000 (or more) in three (or more) banks. One week later borrow $1,000 from the same banks. Make three payments on each loan and then pay off the loan. You have now established a good credit rating and three references.

377 To invest in real estate is to play "Monopoly" with real money.

378 To obtain a building with no cash down, consider giving the seller a loan the *principal* of which *increases* with the CPI (Consumer Price Index). The seller is covered for inflation, and is more inclined to accept nothing down (or low down).

379 Uncle Sam Demands Taxes — This helps to remember the elements of value: Utility, Scarcity, Demand & Transferability.

380 Use about ¼% to ½% of the purchase price per month on an option payment.

381 Use accoustical glass (like shatter-proof glass) or double-pane to eliminate traffic noise.

382 Use equity in one project to leverage into another.

383 Use lead-lined sheetrock (used in recording studios) to stop outside noise.

384 WADED — Five methods of acquiring title to property: Will, Adverse possession, Deed, Estoppel & Descent.

385 We have so much democracy we can't get anything done.

386 We usually undervalue *cash flow* and overvalue *capital gain*.

387 When Joe Smith is buying for another party, it is usually best to write on the Deposit Receipt, "Joe Smith and/or assignee," rather than "nominee."

388 When renting two or more units the tenants tend to balance out each other's behavior. If only one tenant, they would not call the landlord to mention their misdeeds.

389 When selling a property, consider *carrying the first loan* (a purchase money first). The value of the building and equity of the buyer are known facts. It could represent your best investment choice, with positive cash flow, management free, and from a well known security.

390 When you are at the top of your profession you can achieve in an hour what previously took up to a year.

391 WIZARD — A professional with the MOFIA, who helps you along the yellow brick road.

392 Yellow Brick Road — the road that leads to the Bluebird, the Wizard, and the pot of gold (POG).

393 You can depreciate property, not people. If you owned people (slavery) you could depreciate them. This is not moral or legal, so you cannot take a depreciated value of your own life.

MICHEL EYQUEN de MONTAIGNE
French essayist
February 28, 1533 - September 13, 1592

394 You make your money when you 'package' and buy right.

395 You should make at least 3.5 times in salary the amount you spend on your loan payments plus expenses.

396 Yield to the caprices of all and you soon will have nothing to yield at all. —*Aesop*

397 Courage is endurance for one moment more.

398 Peter Principle: To rise up the corporate ladder to finally reach your level of incompetence.

399 Nothing can take the place of persistence. Talent will not; nothing is more common than unsuccessful people with talent. Genius will not; unrewarded genius is almost a proverb. Education will not; the world is full of educated derelicts. Persistence and determination alone are the omnipotent. —*Calvin Coolidge*

400 A real estate partnership may be an excellent investment, but it is not a liquid asset.

401 Beware of analysis paralysis.

402 "Adaptive reuse" done properly is one way to create a fortune. A run-down shopping center is converted to modern office space and high-tech factory with a location near transportation and work force. The property is moderately priced and comes complete with parking.

403 Take no prisoners.

404 You can lead a horse to drink, but you can't make him water.

405 Doers do and teachers tell.

406 Nobody ever went broke underestimating the intelligence of the American public.

407 Resist assumptions, especially your own.

408 If the termites ever stop holding hands, half the buildings in town would collapse.

409 When carrying a loan you can put in a clause, "that each December the payment can be omitted." This is known as the "Santa Clause".

410 I do not choose to be a common man. It is my right to be uncommon ... if I can. I seek opportunity ... not security. I do not wish to be a kept citizen, humbled and dulled by having the state look after me. I want to take the calculated risk; to dream and to build, to fail and to succeed. I refuse to barter incentive for a dole. I prefer the challenges of life to the guaranteed existence; the thrill of fulfillment to the stale calm of utopia. I will not trade freedom for beneficence nor my dignity for a handout. I will never cower before any master nor bend to any threat. It is my heritage to stand erect, proud and unafraid; to think and act for myself; enjoy the benefits of my creations and to face the world boldly and say, This I have done. All this is what it means to be an American. —*Dean Alfange*

411 I asked a friend, who was a submarine commander in World War II, how he prepared for a combat patrol? His reply, "I wrote myself off. If I returned it was a big plus."

412 Earth to Roy ... earth to Roy ... come in ... come in.

413 To help you decide what is important in your life ... all it takes is one good friend, following a minor business reversal ... to blow his brains out.

414 I wish I had drunk more champagne. —*Lord Keynes*

415 God grant me the serenity to accept the things I can not change. Courage to change the things I can and the wisdom to know the difference.

416 It is too late to whet the sword when the trumpet sounds. —*Aesop*

417 You either have been sued or will be.

418 The most painful thing to bear is seeing a mockery made of what one loves. —*Albert Camus*

419 When purchasing a property, never forget deferred maintenance. The maintenance budget for Disneyland is thirty million dollars a year.

420 Soon or late, it is ideas not vested interests, which are dangerous for good or evil. —*John Maynard Keynes*

421 Think preactive rather than reactive.

422 Invest your time, before you invest your money.

423 You can't make an omelette without breaking eggs.

424 When you do finally make your million...many people will think of you as a cash register.

425 When you are concerned about a mistake...consider the eye surgeon who removed the wrong eye.

426 Life is a bitch, and then you die.

427 Cash, note, or "partridge in a pear tree". Take one and all if you have a use...or can convert to cash.

428 Mariners using the first sextant could determine latitude and longitude from two stars within one mile. Using computers we should do so well in selecting the location of a property.

429 I refuse to have a battle of wits with an unarmed person.

MIGUEL de CERVANTES
Spanish novelist
1547 - April 23, 1616

430 Having spent 2 1/2 hours assembling a teak bookcase...it is humbling to note that when done properly it takes 20 minutes. I asked the store manager for more complete instructions and learned that all the screws should be put in position in their special plastic brackets...then tightened with the screwdriver at a 45 degree angle. The moral seems to be to learn all you can before you start a new project. I somehow felt better to learn that a doctor had used nails with destructive results.

431 About 50,000 1/4" drill bits were sold last year. None of the 50,000 people who bought them wanted a 1/4" drill bit. They wanted 50,000 1/4" holes.

432 Having trouble finding certain types of hardware and paint ... try a large boat supply store.

433 A creative mess, is better than tidy idleness.

434 Everybody is entitled to my opinion.

435 The Bishop Mansion in San Francisco has a fire sprinkler system on the *outside*.The sprinklers extend out about two feet from the eaves and help protect the sides from catching fire from an adjacent building. This also helps lower the insurance.

436 If you don't know where you are going ... you're there.

437 A designer friend placed an *empty* one inch conduit underground in a large new development, from *all* businesses to *all* houses. It would then be an easy matter to have a *future* communications video system.

438 If you don't want the money this year ... have the check post-dated to Jan 2nd.

439 Consider a clause: Buyer requires the right to positive cash flow ... it may not be enforceable, but it can help weed out poor deals.

440 When our neighbor's house is on fire, it is time to look to our own. —*Aesop*

441 He couldn't find his way out of a burning telephone booth.
—*John Kockos*

442 So you made $50,000 capital gains on the property you bought four years ago with a no down payment purchase ... How about the $60,000 you spent on mortgage payments, legal fees, taxes, expenses and maintenance?

443 Do you know how to make a small fortune in real estate? Start with a large fortune.

444 An owner of a property spending an average $10 per day on maintenance and repairs for five years can prevent $100,000 worth of time and materials by a contractor ... and possible loss of the property.

445 I hope you get as much pleasure reading my book, as I get spending the money you paid for it.

446 Nothing for nothing.

447 He was born in an obscure village, the child of a peasant woman. He grew up in another village, where He worked in a carpenter shop until He was thirty. Then for three years He was an itinerant preacher. He never wrote a book. He never held an office. He never had a family or owned a home. He didn't go to college. He never visited a big city. He never traveled two hundred miles from the place where He was born. He did none of the things that usually accompany greatness. He had no credentials but Himself. He was only thirty-three when the tide of public opinion turned against Him. His friends ran away. One of them denied Him. He was turned over to His enemies and went through the mockery of a trial. He was nailed to a cross between two thieves. While He was dying ... His executioners gambled for His garments, the only property He had on earth. When He was dead, He was laid in a borrowed grave through the pity of a friend. Nineteen centuries have come and gone, and today He is the central figure of the human race. All the armies that ever marched, all the navies that ever sailed, all the parliaments that ever sat, all the kings that ever reigned, put together, have not affected the life of man on this earth as much as that ...—*One Solitary Life*

448 Thinking of an option, instead of buying, as your first approach to real estate investing . . . is a little like using cinnamon on your breakfast cereal, instead of sugar . . . it is simple, but used by few.

449 Name the most overlooked creative financing technique—Lease/Option

450 Stick with me and you will be wearing potatoes as big as diamonds.

451 Want to control the tenants and building . . . then lease/option. Want to control the building only, then option.

452 Original wiring in old victorian mansions kept a space between the two electrical wires, so that when a rat, or workman, cut through a wire the power would go off . . . but it would not spark and cause a fire.

453 Gresham's Law — Bad money drives out good money.

454 If you want to see an almost perfect example of working with nature in the center of a large city . . . Take the "riverwalk" in San Antonio, Texas.

455 The writer does the most who gives his reader the most knowledge, and takes from him the least time. —*Sidney Smith*

456 To be proud of knowledge, is to be blind with light.

457 He's a good friend that speaks well of us behind our backs.

458 All's lost that is poured into a cracked dish.

459 If you pursue good with labor, the labor passes away, but the good remains; if you pursue evil with pleasure, the pleasure passes, but the evil remains.

460 He that lieth down with dogs, shall rise up with fleas.

461 Slander is the homage which vice pays to virtue.

FRANCIS BACON
English statesman and author
January 22, 1561 - April 9, 1626

462 Every grief has twenty shadows, most of them of your own making.

463 To enjoy a lifetime romance — fall in love with yourself.

464 If the owner of a property does not want to move, and you want to buy ... try a purchase offer with the owner to have a five, or more,year lease with no payments. For example: seller to have right of occupancy for five years. Rental value to be $12,000 per year. Seller to pay no rent for five years, but buyer to have a $60,000 credit to down payment. As one owner properly analysed; I was trying to sell him his own building.

465 Pride goeth before a fall —*Aesop*

466 Try to leave things better than you found them.

467 You bring to real estate investing, as you bring to any endeavor, the sum total of all of your experiences. If it is not working out, then you need a new experience.

468 You will never know how many friends you have, until you own a beachfront penthouse on Maui.

469 Never play the other man's game.

470 Don't put more cash in a speculation than you can afford to lose.

471 To increase the odds on having a counter-offer accepted, consider using odd numbers, e.g., instead of offering $110,000 ... offer $107,940.

472 You don't have to like a person to make a good deal for both parties. Hitler pushed through the "peoples car" ... Volkswagen, and Mussolini had the trains running on time.

473 Money still talks ... but you may have to turn up the volume.

474 An entrepreneur spends 16 hours a day to avoid having to work for someone else for eight hours. —*James Healey*

475 Action is the slave to memory. —*Hamlet*

476 Rather to bear what ills we have, than fly to others that we know not of. —*Hamlet*

477 All income proceeds from capital.

478 CRAP. Creative Reverse Annuity Program.

479 MOUND. MOnumental UNmitigated Disaster.

480 Make no little plans, they have no magic.

481 I eschew obfuscation.

482 The difference between a house and a home is similar to the difference between having sex and making love.

483 Things are seldom what they seem, skim milk masquerades as cream. —*Gilbert and Sullivan*

484 *Donkey can not decide which bale of hay to eat and starves to death. —Aesop's fables*

485 He who is hungry never finds the bread hard.

486 A verbal agreement isn't worth the paper it's written on. —*Sam Goldwyn*

487 If you have a historic building consider donating a "restrictive facade easement" to the federal, state or city government, or a historic foundation for a charitable deduction. The contribution is usually calculated at 15 to 20% of the buildings anticipated value after renovation.

488 Hoist by one's own petard. To be blown up by one's own bomb.

489 If anything good happens I will take credit, if anything bad happens it will be your fault.

490 You may get outbid at a real estate auction ... you will for sure occasionaly be outbid in the auction of life.

491 One movie mogul when confronted with new business schemes, always had one question: Does it sell tickets?

492 My take home pay won't take me home anymore.

493 Time is a subtle psychological factor in your enjoyment of property. If you plan on keeping a property for 10, 20 or 30 years ... a leaky roof, broken window, or other problems can be amortized over the total period of ownership ... these identical problems are greatly magnified when in a hotel room for one night.

494 There can be no question that the place for the general in battle is where he can see the battle and get the odor of it in his nostrils.
—*Gen. James M. Gavin*

495 One man's microscope is another man's telescope.

496 Toxic waste produced, by American industry, equals about 300 pounds per year for every man, woman and child.

497 I am easy ... all I want is compliance with my wishes after reasonable discussion.

498 Everything in place, and a place for everything.

499 Useful output divided by useful input equals efficiency.

500 We have so many social problems, because people have the opposite of what they want.

501   Every fake in the world needs a real thing to imitate.

502   More blessed to give than to receive. You take the blessing, I'll take the money.

503   Poor people are present oriented. Rich people are future oriented.

504   The average person spends as much buying cars as they do on houses . . . only they buy more cars.

505   His mind was unmortgaged.

506   A hotel executive's reason for being in touch with his employees and their problems . . . he estimated traveling an average of 500 miles per day and visiting every hotel in his chain.

507   Leverage is the use of a smaller investment to generate a larger profit.

508   Even a fool is wise . . . when it is too late! —*Aesop*

509   He who tries too much doesn't do anything.

510   Appearances are deceiving.

511   He that can compose himself, is wiser than he that composes books.

512   Do not be breaking your shin on a stool that's not in your way.

513   Words may show a man's wit, but actions his meaning.

514   Solomon made a book of proverbs, but a book of proverbs never made a Solomon.

515   The way to do is to be. —*Lao-Tse*

516   Discover new truths of old creation.

517 I prefer honest arrogance to hypocritical humility.
—*Frank Lloyd Wright*

518 Happiness is the pursuit of excellence within the limits of your own capability

519 Equity is the dollar amount of ownership, the difference between fair market value of property and existing loans.

520 Winners & Losers — A winner knows what he will do if he loses, a loser only knows what he will do if he wins.

521 When directed, and focused, two watts of sun power can burn through steel.

522 Don't take life too seriously . . . you won't get out of it alive.

523 Don't eat the seedcorn.

524 Even when the bird walks we see that he has wings. —*Lemoine*

525 If you can say nothing good, then say nothing.

526 A very quick and easy way to obtain a down payment for a property you would like to purchase, is to create a second note from the equity in a property that you own.

527 To have a million and owe two million is to be a negative millionaire.

528 Wealth is large results from small efforts. Poverty is small results from large efforts. Capital is the means to achieve desired results.

529 A little pot and soon hot. —*Cervantes*

530 The used key is always bright. —*Benjamin Franklin*

WILLIAM SHAKESPEARE
English dramatist
April 26, 1564 - April 23, 1616

531   Nature abhors a vacuum, and so do squatters.

532   A man is rich in proportion to the number of things he can do without —*Thoreau*

533   The best loan is always obtained from the seller lending the money. This is called a "purchase money loan", and is indicated on the purchase agreement in "seller to carry" clause (seller "to take back paper").

534   Thomas Edison was asked by a skeptic how he could justify 1,000 unsuccessful experiments on a single project. Edison replied cheerfully: "Now we know 1,000 ways that won't work."

535   Fission and fusion are two basic systems of the universe. Fission splits, fusion joins. Using lasers a force field, or "invisible bottle," is developed with enough power to create a small star. Invisible bottles can be created with the power of your mind. To produce bright ideas.

536   Many go out for wool and come home shorn. —*Aesop*

537   Don't stay home and mope, get out and grope.

538   One way to interest the seller in an option is to increase the amount of the option money each month. You could start with say $1,000, then increase to $2,000, $3,000 etc.

539   To lower the federal def i cit: expenditures must be lowered, and/or taxes must be raised. A property owner must act in a parallel manner. Increase the income and/or lower the expenses.

540   Before you say the tenth story condo is too expensive, compare it with a similar house raised 100 feet in the air having a comparable view.

541   If you must close escrow, or finalize the sale of a property, but you feel that you are being treated unfairly regarding monies ... there is a way you can submit your check "under protest". You can then sue for damages after you own the property. The author has done this successfully.

542 Two basic rules of leadership and management:
(1) Delegate authority on tasks that others can do as well or better than yourself.
(2) Don't lose control.

543 He exercises his mind jumping to conclusions.

544 To take action is more important than to attend another positive attitude seminar.

545 TICLE. Tenant in common lease. A master lease can be divided into sections with exclusive rights of occupancy.

546 A friend and long time resident on Maui, pointed out that a million dollar property directly on the beach, with an unobstructed view, would be worth only about half as much, one block away from the beach, or even across the street. From personal observations I believe this is accurate for Rio de Janiero, Sydney, Fiji, Monaco, Grand Bahama Island, Capetown, Palm Beach, and in fact any world famous beach area.

547 In talks with other authors I note the books they have never written always excel the one I have in hand.

548 Before you tear out the floor to clear plugged plumbing try renting a "Kinetic Water Ram". It is a high compression air blast gun manufactured by General Wire Spring Co. in McKees Rocks, Pennsylvania.

549 For the security of tenants no new building should be constructed without at least considering a built in closed circuit television system with cameras aimed at all points of entrance. You may not be able to stop a problem, but at least you can see it coming.

550 The only difference between rape and seduction is salesmanship.

551 His only polish was on his shoes.

552 You could create a man with more backbone than his, if you carved a spine out of a banana.

553 Great architecture gives you the most bang for the buck.

554 NIH. Not invented here. A syndrome that rejects all thought not done in house.

555 2 for 1 rule. When establishing a thermocycle system for the natural flow of air through a building. The outlet on the top should be twice as large as the intake port on the bottom.

556 If you give me the responsibility, then give me the authority.

557 Res Judicata. The thing has been decided.

558 Envy shoots at others and wounds herself.

559 The heart of a fool is in his mouth, but the mouth of a wise man is in his heart.

560 What the fool does in the end, the wise man does in the beginning.

561 A little explained, a little endured, a little forgiven, the quarrel is cured.

562 One should know a horse by its speed, an ox by its burden, a cow by its milk, and a wise man by his speech.

563 Industry pays debts, despair increases them.

564 People who are wrapped up in themselves make small packages.

565 His mouth costs him nothing, for he never opens it but at other's expense.

FRANCOIS DUC DE LA ROCHEFOUCAULD
French moralist and writer
December 15, 1613 - March 17, 1680

566 Fools need advice most, but only wise men are the better for it.

567 Quoin. The bricks, or stone, forming the corner of a wall.

568 As said when receiving an abusive tirade: Do you need me for this conversation?

569 A camel is a horse designed by a committee.

570 I have a friend who thought he was doing fairly well in business making $4,000 a month ... the only problem was that he spent $5,000 a month.

571 One reason for the beauty of Carmel by the Sea in California are the ordinances that prohibit the cutting of trees, and the erecting of neon or plastic signs.

572 It is true art to conceal art.

573 Before you die you can count on: a flat tire, running out of gas, falling down, a dentist and doctor bill, a leaky faucet, a bruise, a stopped drain, a hole in your sock, being late, losing a friend, a financial error, etc. Play it cool.

574 Don't pop out of the same hole twice.

575 A person who does not read good books has no advantage over the person who can't read them. —*Mark Twain*

576 Better the devil you know, than the angel you don't. —*Fred Lorenzino*

577 Good judgement comes from experience, and experience comes from poor judgement.

578 Parkinson's Law. Your work will expand to fill the time.

579 One man's opinion is that the most creative financing is the option.

580 An excellent product that seems to be virtually unknown is the earthquake *gas valve*. It is installed on the intake gas line to your building. It works with an internal pendulum switch that can only move with a violent shake of the gas pipe. It costs in the $130 range, and takes about an hour and a half to install.

581 It is possible to have plumbing in perfect working order, and return from a vacation and find your tub, or sink completely stopped. The reason is the scale on the inside of the pipe becomes dry, breaks off, and forms a plug to block the flow of water. The solution is keep your scale moist.

582 Need more outdoor space, or a sun deck? Consider a porte-co-chere, a covered carriage (or auto) entrance leading to a courtyard. The roof of which can be useable space.

583 The greatest waste ... is the difference between what you are, and what you could be.

584 People have the ability to major in minor things.

585 You need a Phd in common sense.

586 You must put will do with want too.

587 On a property you want to buy ... have an appraisal based on the remodelling you *plan* in the future. Then offer as down payment to the seller the cost of the completed remodel work.

588 Consider a mortgage broker when you need a loan. They are motivated professionals (in most cases) and may obtain the loan without you ever seeing the lender.

589 Determine pro-rations on every deal before you close it.

590 Cash on cash is equal to the cash flow (net income after debt service) as a percent of the down payment.

591 You can make a negotiated offer on a foreclosure property, because many times the principals are not talking to each other.

592 When the seller is not hurting for cash, it is always worth trying to obtain seller financing. No money or low down is possible when the seller knows he is dealing with a professional with a track record, good credit, and a logical deal.

593 Remember that everyday your building is deteriorating. "Ashes to ashes, dust to dust", unless you do something about it.

594 The ignorant despise what is precious only because they cannot understand it. —*Aesop*

595 Look for corridors of moderately priced property, between established areas of high priced property.

596 A legal contract gives the executor of your estate the ability to do his job.

597 A vacant lot with approved building plans could easily have double the fair market value of the land alone. If you also have signed long term leases from blue chip companies to accompany the plans ... you should probably be writing this book.

598 The two rules for forecasting interest rates are:
(1) Don't do it
(2) Or do it often.

599 A multi-millionaire friend lost over $200,000 in one day on his airline stock. His response, "No big deal, I didn't work for the money anyway."

600 He has all the qualities of a dog except loyalty.

601 Step by step the ladder is ascended.

JEAN-JACQUES ROUSSEAU
Swiss-French philosopher
June 28, 1712 - July 2, 1778

602 Separate the wheat from the chaff.

603 Just as in flying there is a power curve, i.e. you must maintain a certain speed and altitude, or crash. There is in real estate a power curve of income and expenses. Saddled with too great a debt and you are doomed to crash.

604 A question too rarely asked of oneself, particularly on the first real estate venture . . . How much can I borrow and still eat?

605 Stop the world . . . I want to get off.

606 A fairly new concept in real estate is "proprietary interests", e.g., a large tract of land, say A 3,000 acre mountain resort is divided between 2,000 equal owners. It is similar to "tenants in common," with each party having an undivided interest in the entire project.

607 Whenever you are getting too puffed up with how many great deals you are making, how much money you made, and how smart you are . . . just consider the significance forty years from now.

608 If you think education is expensive, try ignorance. —*Derek Bok, president, Harvard University*

609 Better . . . is better.

610 High interest rates are good news for savers, and bad news for borrowers.

611 Hereditaments: being inherited, be it corporeal, incorporeal, real, personal, or mixed.

612 You cut the pie in half. I will choose the half.

613 Raison d'etre. The reason of existing.

614 Good architecture plus good business, makes good sense.

615 If you are in a joint tenancy with right of survivorship and you want out, you may be able to convert to a tenants in common. One method involves deeding yourself a quit-claim deed.

616 We often mistake notoriety for fame. —*Aesop*

617 Rather to be a burning meteor, than a dead star.

618 Civilization is the result of staying in one place. By that standard one of the most primitive tribes is the Australian aboriginies who are on constant "walk-about". They carry not even blankets, but use dogs to stay warm. A "four dog night" is particularly cold.

619 In Africa a tribe suffering losses from warring neighbors of its most attractive women ... disfigured the women so they were less desirable. A few generations later the reason for the disfigurement was forgotten, and Ubangi lips became a mark of beauty. Today's kitsch is tomorrow's antique.

620 Hobson's choice. A choice without an alternative. Named after Thomas Hobson, circa 1544—1631, of Cambridge, England. When renting horses he obliged each customer to take the horse nearest the stable door, or none at all.

621 A meeting is not a policy. —*Dean Atcheson*

622 The profound can be superficial, and the superficial can be profound. —*Bill Moyers*

623 Learn to manage money, or it will manage you.

624 You will find your own good in the good of the whole community.

625 On Maui, the Valley Isle disposal trucks have painted on their sides, "We guarantee our service, or double your garbage back." I have known seminar speakers who could use this motto.

626 Even experts tend to overlook or minimize maintenance reserves and the total costs of loans.

627 In battle, if you do not win, the individual has three choices: to be killed, wounded or taken prisoner ... there are parallels in investing.

628 Observing my interest in a project, an Australian friend commented, "Mate, you'r all over that like a bucket of grubs."

629 Don't worry if the horse is blind, load the wagon.

630 If you are having fun, the people around you will have fun.

631 If not now ... when?

632 A rising tide lifts all boats.

633 PLU. People like us.

634 TINFLA. There is no free lunch anymore.

635 You want real estate that is "user friendly".

636 Lenin's dictum was that the capitalists will eventually sell the rope that will hang them.

637 He's a legend in his own mind.

638 I am the master of my fate; I am the captain of my soul. —*Henley*

639 Part of winning is not being afraid to lose.

640 One mark of a professional is to hire another professional.

641 A change of scene does not change one's character. —*Aesop*

642 A slip of the foot you may soon recover, but a slip of the tongue you may never get over.

643 Three may keep a secret, if two of them are dead. —*Benjamin Franklin*

644 There are three things extremely hard: steel, a diamond and to know one's self.

645 Patience is a tree whose root is bitter, but its fruit is very sweet.

646 In a calm sea every man is a pilot.

647 Do you seek ultimate truth? O blind man, in a dark room, looking for a black cat that isn't there.

648 A mouse must not think to cast a shadow like an elephant.

649 He has good judgement, who relies not wholly on his own.

650 The gown is hers that wears it, and the world is his that enjoys it.

651 The greatest and sublimest power is often simple patience.

652 Wisdom is a good purchase, though we pay dear for it.

653 He most lives who thinks most, feels noblest, and acts best.

654 Oh the joy of young ideas painted on the mind. In warm glowing colors fancy spreads on objects not yet known, when all is new, and all is lovely. —*Hannah More*

655 A questioning student is more important than an answering teacher.

656 I have deemed it more honorable and more profitable too, to set a good example than to follow a bad one. —*Thomas Jefferson*

657 The ability to think and act are the qualities which translate dead knowledge into living wisdom.

658 The mark of an educated man is the ability to make a reasoned guess on the basis of insufficient information.
—*A. Lawrence Lowell*, former president of Harvard University.

659 Courage consists not in blindly overlooking danger, but in seeing it, and conquering it. —*Jean Paul Richter*

660 Nonsense, that would never be noticed from a trotting horse.
—*Emily Kimbrough*

661 The way to enjoy anything in life is to know that you can get along without it.

662 The world is coming to an end tonight. The reply of Ralph Waldo Emerson, "I can get along without it."

663 What do you call a liberal who has been mugged? A conservative.

664 This and better will do. —*Capt. Nick Gabriel, Harbor Light*

665 It requires more than wings to be an eagle. —*Aesop*

666 Wit talks most, when she has least to say, and reason interrupts not her career.

667 Contentment is the philosopher's stone, which turns all it touches into gold; the poor man is rich with it, the rich man is poor without it.

668 A harvest of peace is produced from a seed of contentment.

669 An old man continues to be young in two things - love of money and love of life.

670 One good plan that works is better than a hundred doubtful ones.
—*Aesop*

671 Keep conscience clear, then never fear.

THOMAS PAINE
American political essayist
January 29, 1737 - June 8, 1809

672   Adversity makes a man wise, not poor.

673   There was never a good knife made of bad steel.

674   A bad habit is like good bread: better broken than kept.

675   Who will not keep a penny, shall never have many.

676   Benefits, like flowers, please most when they are fresh.

677   Give me a condor's quill! Give me Vesuvius' crater for an inkstand! ... To produce a mighty book, you must choose a mighty theme. —*Melville*

678   True courage is to do without witnesses everything that one is capable of doing before all the world. —*La Rouchefoucauld.*

679   A feeble man can see the farms that are fenced and tilled, the houses that are built. The strong man sees the possible houses and farms. His eye makes estates as fast as the sun breeds clouds. —*Emerson*

680   He is the greatest artist who has embodied in the sum of his works, the greatest number of the greatest ideas. —*John Ruskin*

681   As for myself, I want to do my work well ... and to die well. —*Unknown French girl*

682   Master yourself and you can master anything.

683   Where there is no vision, the people perish. —*Proverbs 29:18*

684   One thing at a time ... appreciate the moment. —*Isamu Noguchi*

685   We search for happiness in every quarter ... except within us.

686   Will Rogers never met a man he didn't like, with the possible exception of Wiley Post.

687   Silence creates a space for the mind.

688   Yesterday is but a dream and tomorrow only a vision. Look well to this day.

689   The sooner you make new friends, the sooner you will have old ones.
—*Dr. Eric Berne*

690   A clean mouth and an honest hand will take a man through any land.

691   Better a dry morsel and quietness therewith, than a home full of feasting with strife.

692   The greatest wealth is contentment with a little.

693   A blind man will not thank you for a looking-glass.

694   One pair of heels is often worth two pair of hands.

695   Discontents do arise from our desires oftener than from our needs.

696   If wisdom's ways you wisely seek, five things observe with care: of whom you speak, to whom you speak, and how, and when, and where.

697   Temper is so good a thing that we should never lose it.

698   Quid pro quo. Something for something.

699   Now is always beginning.

700   Worry is like a rocking chair. It gives you something to do but doesn't get you anywhere.

701 Having trouble with tenants that do not want a condo conversion because they can't afford it? Offer to put up a down payment of 20% if they will qualify for an 80% loan. You receive the loan proceeds (tenant pays all expenses) and because you have put up the 20% down (you actually just extended credit since you own the building) you have applied equity participation (tenants in common or other) to your own building.

702 Tomorrow has been cancelled due to lack of interest.

703 Apothecaries would not give pills in sugar unless they were bitter.

704 The worst wheel of the cart makes the most noise.

705 A quiet conscience sleeps in thunder, but rest and guilt live far asunder.

706 Fools laugh at others; wise men at themselves.

707 It is not having an eye for faults, but for beauties, that constitutes the real critic.

708 If misfortune comes, she brings along the bravest virtues.

709 A gem is not polished without rubbing, nor a man perfected without trials.

710 Wealth is not his that has it, but his that enjoys it.

711 If your head is wax, don't walk in the sun.

712 Cast no dirt into the well that gives you water.

713 There are many do it yourself people. You ask them to do something and they say, "Do it yourself."

714 He drank a bottle of varnish by mistake yesterday. He had a horrible death ... but a lovely finish.

WILLIAM BLAKE
English poet and artist
November 28, 1757 - August 12, 1827

715   What you don't know you can always learn.

716   Men who do things that count never stop to count them.

717   Time waits for no one.

718   It is thinking about the load that makes one tired.

719   Not what you do, but how you do it.

720   May you have warm words on a cold evening. A full moon on a dark night. And the road downhill all the way home. —*An Irish toast*

721   A thing done right today means no trouble tomorrow.

722   Some men grow, others swell.

723   May the road rise up to meet you, may the wind be always at your back, may the sun shine warm upon your face, and the rains fall soft upon your fields. And until we meet again, may God hold you in the palm of his hand, but never close his fist too tightly. —*An Irish toast*

724   Every blade of grass has its share of the dews of heaven.

725   Beware of little expenses: a small leak will sink a great ship.

726   Sell not the bear's skin before you have caught him.

727   Wise men learn by other men's mistakes, fools by their own.

728   Few things seem so possible as they are till they are attempted.

729   If you think twice before you speak once, you will speak twice the better for it.

730 These are three faithful friends — an old wife, an old dog, and ready money.

731 The more you know, the more you realize you don't know.

732 Wisdom is knowing what to do next.

733 Small minds discuss persons. Average minds discuss events. Great minds discuss ideas.

734 Too often we despise the very things that are most useful to us. —*Aesop*

735 Every day gives you another chance.

736 Every time you speak, your mind is on parade.

737 The real essence of work is concentration.

738 Talk less, think more.

739 When I die I'm going to leave you all the money you owe me.

740 I care not so much what I am in the opinion of others as what I am in my own; I would be rich of myself and not of borrowing. —*Montaigne*

741 There is far more opportunity than there is ability. —*Thomas Edison*

742 He who does something at the head of one regiment will eclipse him who does nothing at the head of a hundred. —*Abraham Lincoln*

743 Never esteem anything as of advantage to you that shall make you break your word or lose your self respect. —*Marcus Aurelius*

744 Let nothing disturb thee; let nothing dismay thee; all things pass; God never changes. —*St Teresa of Avila*

745 We shall have no better conditions in the future if we are satisfied with all those we have at present. —*Thomas A. Edison*

746 Fear knocked at the door. Faith answered. No one was there.

747 If everyone swept his own doorstep, then the whole wide world would be clean.

748 Those who cannot remember the past are condemned to repeat it. —*George Santayana*

749 Liars are not believed even when they tell the truth. —*Aesop*

750 The best thinking has been done in solitude. The worst has been done in turmoil. —*Thomas A. Edison*

751 I have always wanted to deal with everyone I meet candidly and honestly. If I have made any assertion not warranted by facts, and it is pointed out to me. I will withdraw it cheerfully. —*Abraham Lincoln*

752 A purchaser of property is well advised (I would urge you) to have the seller verify that the leases are correct and/or send an *estoppel statement* (letter) to all of the tenants with a self-addressed stamped return envelope. The letter would ask that they fill in the blanks as to the terms and conditions of the lease, and to sign and return it.

753 If you are getting all you ask for, maybe you are not asking for enough.

754 Spouse explaining how to afford the luxurious estate with all the ammenities, "If I spend it, he has to make it."

ROBERT BURNS
Scottish poet
January 25, 1759 - July 21, 1796

755   Having dealt with about a thousand tenants I estimate about one per cent to be candidates for retroactive birth control ... and they no doubt felt the same about the landlord.

756   The author has six fountains in his backyard ... they create a sound not unlike crashing surf ... this was the intention. A comparatively inexpensive solution in lieu of buying beach front property.

757   To create a natural antique green patina on your fountain let a few quarts of buttermilk stand in the still water for two or three weeks. A true Roy's rot.

758   I was so uninformed I thought Sherlock Holmes was a housing project.

759   You can bond around a lien. Your equity should be about double the lien. A friend had a bonding agent provide a bond against an IRS tax lien on a property in order to have a "clean deal" for the new buyer.

760   Your ideas in as much as they have any merit, have previously been considered and rejected.

761   Half of something is better than one hundred per cent of nothing.

762   Failure,failure and failure makes success. It might take three restaurant failures to make a success. You pick up ten new steady customers with each failure, and it takes about forty to be a success.

763   A friend is someone you want around after you find the one you want.

764   Let bygones be bygones. Yes, but it usually applies to negative events. Be sure to remember the good bygones. The purpose of work is to create good bygones.

765   A friend told of two words, told to him by a wiser and older man, that changed his demeanor. Quiet strength.

766 Our enemies speak of our lust for world domination and power. In a lifetime I have yet to meet the first person from San Diego, New York, Beverly Hills, Newport Beach, San Francisco, Dallas, St Petersburg, et al, who wanted to move to Stalingrad.

767 The eye of the master will do more work than his hand.

768 Who never climbed, never fell.

769 A bird is known by its note, a man by his talk.

770 Better suffer a great evil than do a little one.

771 Faults are thick where love is thin.

772 He bears poverty very ill who is ashamed of it.

773 He that sows iniquity shall reap sorrow.

774 Money is a good servant, but a dangerous master.

775 It is madness for a sheep to treat for peace with a wolf.

776 Better a lean peace than a fat victory.

777 The poor have little, beggers none; the rich too much, enough not one.

778 Laziness travels so slowly that poverty soon overtakes him.

779 He who seeks a compliment sometimes discovers the truth. —*Aesop*

780 The purpose of investment is to protect us from the darkness that enshrouds our future. —*John Maynard Keynes*

781 Behind every stupid idea is a grain of truth.

782 If you want to have a handle on how your life is going ... try writing your own epitaph.

783 One man's house can be another man's home.

784 A bank can borrow money from the Federal Reserve Bank. They can then lend the money to their customers. If they borrow at say 11% and loan it out at 18%, the interest spread is 7%, which represents the gross profit. If for each dollar on deposit they can borrow on the order of ten dollars, then if they lend it all out the gross profit is 70%.

785 You can act, or react; you can control, or be controlled.

786 I was worried about my shoes until I met a man with no feet.

787 Relativity is easier to understand than the Federal Tax Code, because God is not malicious.

788 If you don't risk, you risk even more.

789 If you can imagine it, you can do it. —*William A. Ward*

790 A "letter of intent" when signed by both parties, can tie up even a large project for a few days. It is an excellent way of "getting there firstest with the mostest." It allows you breathing room, and a chance to get your act together.

791 Much water goes by the mill that the miller knows not of.

792 A little debt makes a debtor, but a great one an enemy.

793 An ass is but an ass, though laden with gold.

794 First deserve, and then desire.

795 If you wish to know the character of the prince, look at his ministers; if you wish to understand the man, look at his friends; if you wish to know the father, observe his son.

796 A fault once denied, is twice committed.

797 He that would please all, and himself too, understands what he cannot do.

798 A man without money is a bow without an arrow.

799 Poverty wants some things, luxury many things, and avarice all things.

800 He that is of the opinion that money will do everything may well be suspected of doing everything for money.

801 Do you have a lease or note, you wish to extend? Start negotiating at least three months before it expires. You don't want to be "under the gun" to accept new terms on the expiration date.

802 And so we plough along, as the fly said to the ox. —*Longfellow*

803 A crust eaten in peace is better than a banquet partaken in anxiety. —*Aesop*

804 The good news is that you obtained a court judgement against a debtor, the bad news is that you can't find him to collect. Your judgement is just a piece of paper.

805 If you can't find the co-owner of your property and you wish to remove their name from the records, consider a "petition to the court" to have the name legally removed.

806 When purchasing a single family home, or other property, that has an "in-law" apartment with the income included on the property statement ... be sure that the unit is legal, and conforms to zoning. It is best to have the information in writing from the owner, as well as checking with the city building department.

807 If you can extend the close of escrow, or the transfer of title, as well as the down payment for three months . . . you have in effect created an option to buy for three months. In that length of time you can line up all of your ducks, and know if you want to go, or no go.

808 He who spits into the eye of the wind, spits into his own eye.

809 Better to be alone than in bad company.

810 For age and want save while you may, no morning sun lasts a whole day.

811 A wise man will desire no more than what he may get justly, use soberly, distribute cheerfully and leave contentedly.

812 A man without courage is a knife without a blade.

813 Better is a poor and wise child, than an old and foolish king.

814 It costs more to revenge injuries than to bear them.

815 He that makes himself an ass must not take it ill if men ride him.

816 There is nothing so eloquent as a rattlesnake's tail.

817 Search others for their virtues, thyself for thy vices.

818 You don't understand a thing until you love it. —*Goethe*

819 One of my best friends made an offer on four hotels in Hawaii. His plan was to time share the individual rooms and suites. He put up five million dollars worth of his own property, to secure a two million dollar loan for the down payment. The offer was ratified, and he proceeded to obtain a new first loan, and have the time share documents executed. He was not able to complete the transaction, and had to sell his properties to raise the two million he borrowed. A real disaster. A simple option for three months would have limited his losses to only the option money.

ANDREW JACKSON
President of the United States, 1829 - 1837
March 15, 1767 - June 8, 1845

820 For a start check three things in real estate: income, growth, and tax advantages.

821 One man with courage is a majority. —*Andrew Jackson*

822 A rough rule of thumb is to look for about 10% of the property value as a tax shelter.

823 Buy a $100,000 note at 9% interest per annum, and sell, or renegotiate, at 12%. A tidy $3,000 a year profit.

824 Many may share in the labors but not in the spoils. —*Aesop*

825 Yesterday, today was tomorrow.

826 Why tax shelter what isn't taxable?

827 Closing the mouth opens the mind.

828 Read 10 pages a day and you have read 12 books in a year.

829 The taxes on my net income have been gross.

830 The fundamental question is not shelter for your income, but rather having income to shelter.

831 No decision is a decision.

832 Expect nothing and you will never be dissapointed.

833 Assume a virtue if you have it not.

834 Neurotic entitlement is the exact opposite of repairing leaky faucets.

835 You'll never become a 300 hitter unless you take your bat off your shoulder.

836 Experience is a hard teacher because she gives the test first, the lesson afterwards.

837 There is no "I" in team.

838 If you don't play to win, why keep score?

839 When you're through learning you're through.

840 Don't throw the ball before you have it.

841 Nobody ever became a ballplayer by walking after the ball.

842 A wish for a mind unafraid to travel, even though the trail be not blazed.

843 Give not that which is holy unto the dogs, neither cast your pearls before swine, lest they trample them under their feet, and turn again and rend you. —*St. Matthew 7:6*

844 When poverty comes in at the door, love flies out the window. —*17th Century anonymous*

845 A fool and his money are soon parted. —*16th Century, anonymous*

846 How much do you want for your $10,000 note at 8%, due in full in 9 years? It is mathematically exactly equal to 50% of the note, or $5,000, if paid in cash now. Not clear, then review the Present Value of $1 tables.

847 To have a friend you must first be one.

848 Happiness is not knowing enough to understand the problem.

849 One divided by zero is infinity. The author has put zero down payment on a property, and received a $6,000 sales commission. The technique used overlapping deeds of trust as security. The leverage was infinite.

850 A combat admiral speaking of the Marines at Iwo Jima, "Uncommon valor was a common virtue."

851 Paranoia is the unreasonable idea that people are out to get you. Narapoia is the unreasonable idea that people are benevolent. It is a delusionary belief adhered to in the face of all evidence to the contrary.

852 You feel better about paying your taxes as you watch the Blue Angels (Navy jet pilots) do a "starburst" at five thousand feet.

853 Be a laser beam, not a weak flashlight.

854 Simplify, simplify,simplify. —*Thoreau at Walden Pond*

855 Asked of a new president of a restaurant chain, "How did you take your company from near bankruptcy, to a top firm that just had a stock split." Answer, "I just simplified everything."

856 Life is a shipwreck, but we must not forget to sing in the lifeboats. —*Voltaire*

857 I have met the enemy and it is us. —*Pogo*

858 Neither a borrower nor a lender be.

859 Hope for the best, but prepare for the worst.

860 You can't lose 'em all.

861 You only have to deal with about one hundred people in your lifetime to be successful.

SIR WALTER SCOTT
English novelist
August 15, 1771 - September 21, 1832

862 John F Kennedy quoting a sage, "An error doesn't become a mistake until you fail to correct it."

863 Everyday is New Year's eve.

864 Everybody takes back paper except the dealer.

865 A bathtub should never be in the bathroom. —*John Paci*

866 This is not practice, this is reality.

867 If you have two property appraisals more than 5% apart, then get a third.

868 If you own an unbuildable lot, consider asking the city to create a "tot-lot" or "vest-pocket park." if you give it to the city it should count as a charitable contribution for tax purposes.

869 Sanborn fire maps used by insurance companies contain useful lot and building information.

870 When you have two or more people that are to be paid monthly on a Deed of Trust you can have one deed and two or more notes. The note payments can be equal or unequal, but the notes all have the same priority since there is only one deed securing the notes.

871 One definition of a co-signer: Any schmuck with a ball-point pen.

872 Action equals reaction. —*Newton*

873 Luther Burbank estimated that he pulled a million cactus spines from his fingers, during 15 years spent developing an edible cactus for cattle.

874 Emulate the diamond . . . a hunk of coal that made good under pressure.

875 Have a plan and work your plan.

876 Education with motivation is the shortest distance between poverty and wealth.

877 Grasp at the shadow and lose the substance. —*Aesop*

878 You have more problems being satisfied with too little, than striving for too much.

879 Photocopy all rent checks and important documents and put in a fire-proof safe. It is inexpensive insurance against future problems.

880 Top attorneys read over a complicated legal document as many as ten times.

881 Are you worried about your problems? In two years you will have a new set of problems.

882 A garage door with an open, metal grillwork offers the advantage of light, air circulation, and a sense of security, as you can see in before entering.

883 When you want to buy, or trade into another house . . . the safest procedure is to sell your existing home first.

884 Will interest rates go up, or down? Yes, but not right away.

885 Knowledge of the market is more art than science.

886 One of the advantages of having good background knowledge, is that when a deal finally does come . . . you will be able to recognize it.

887 Better a hen today, than an egg tomorrow.

888 Lead by example.

889 It is better to bend than to break. —*Aesop*

890 All the world's wisdom . . . condensed:
1. Never play cards with a man named DOC.
2. Never eat lunch at a place called MOM'S
3. Never sleep with someone whose problems are greater than your own.

891 When you sit down at a poker table, look around you. If you don't see the sucker, get up. You're it!

892 There are times when you should look for trouble. Better to replace a five cent washer, than a hundred dollar faucet.

893 Bankers are like bookies. They are always "laying off" their bets, i.e., matching assets to liabilities. They borrow long, and lend short.

894 The empty vessel giveth a greater sound than the full barrel.
—*John Lyly*

895 In God we trust . . . all others pay cash.

896 Whatever is worth doing at all, is worth doing well. —*Chesterfield*

897 Magnificent promises often end in paltry performances. —*Aesop*

898 He jests at scars , that never felt a wound. —*Shakespeare*

899 Lead, follow, or get out of the way.

900 An oil executive when asked his secret to success, "We drill more holes."

901 RAF. Ready, aim ,fire.

902 While congress debated feasability . . . Teddy Roosevelt's engineers were building the Panama Canal.

903 One of the top car salesmen is known to send out 13,000 greeting cards per month.

VICTOR HUGO
French novelist
February 26, 1802 - May 22, 1885

904 We need more monomaniacs with a mission.

905 MBWA. Management by wandering around.

906 A Nobel laureate's reason for success in discovering an obscure brain hormone, "We ground up more pig brains."

907 Give me a fish and I eat today, show me how to fish and I can eat forever.

908 Agreements are thought out opportunities for taking responsibilities.

909 The brain can absorb only what the seat can tolerate.

910 When you are frustrated by delays on your building project, consider the 22 years and 22,000 workers needed to complete the Taj Mahal.

911 Flood zones should be disclosed to new purchasers. An area that floods every hundred years usually does not have a significant effect on the price. Unless the flood is to occur at the close of escrow.

912 Study and learn and the time will come to use it. —*Abraham Lincoln*

913 Good luck is something you make, bad luck is something you endure.

914 It's not the trophy but the race; it's not the quarry but the chase.

915 You may be unhappy with real estate, but better rich and unhappy, than poor and unhappy.

916 There was a great greyhound racer called "Whitey". He was great until he caught the rabbit. He never won another race.

917 A proverb is a short sentence based on long experience. —*Cervantes*

918 When Dr. Theodore K. Lee was asked by a dental student the secret of dental surgery? He replied, "Cut the meat away."

919 A drop of reason to a flood of words. —*Benjamin Franklin*

920 Power and violence are opposites, where one rules absolutely, the other is absent. —*Hannah Arendt*

921 Seek simplicity and distrust it. —*Alfred North Whitehead*

922 Wisdom is oftimes nearer when we stoop than when we soar.
—*William Wordsworth*

923 *How to stay out of trouble by avoiding the four "D's":*
1. *Drugs*
2. *Debt*
3. *Divorce*
4. *Disease.*
—*Dr. George David*

924 When put to the fire, the steel in a Samurai sword either melts, or is tempered and strengthened.

925 When your neighbor is out of work it is a recession, when you are out of work it is a depression.

926 A decision must be judged according to the information available at the time the decision was made. It is possible to have a bad decision with a good result. An example of the latter is the decision to mortgage one's home then bet the proceeds on Keno, and win.

927 After-tax income is not the same as tax-free income. One is after paying, the latter is never paying taxes. Also "tax-free" may mean deferred taxes, or no federal taxes, and yet there may still be state taxes.

928 Rather than suffer the severe pain of a "commissionectomy" . . . your broker may consider "carrying paper" for six months.

929 There are no stupid questions, only stupid answers.

930 Advertising costs, publicity is free.

931 Where you are now is owned by someone. You can't escape reality or realty.

932 From unhappy experience it is advised that you know exactly where your maintenance fee is going, who paid for it, and for what. You want a monthly report, and the right to inspect the books. You also want to know if a maintenance reserve is established for painting, new roof, et al. Remember it's your money.

933 The difference between a diplomat and a lady: When a diplomat says "yes" he means maybe. When he says "maybe" he means yes. If he says "no" he's not a diplomat.
When a lady says "no" she means maybe. When she says "maybe" she means yes. If she says "yes" she's no lady.

934 There have been cases where tenants involved in an injunction to stop a demolition, had their building demolished during the trial's lunch hour recess.

935 The author has drawn up contracts that the other party did not think were fair. When I mentioned that I would accept a reversal of the terms, and would take their position ... their arguments collapsed.

936 Concerning paying a high price for real estate. The inscription on a World War I monument to the South Africans killed in action at the Somme: Their ideal is our legacy. Their sacrifice our inspiration.

937 It is not the crook in modern business that we fear, but the honest man who does not know what he is doing. —*Owen D. Young*

938 Love is an ocean of emotions, entirely surrounded by expenses.
—*Lord Dewar*

939 It is better to understand little than to misunderstand a lot.
—*Anatole France*

940 No amount of experimentation can prove me right, yet one experiment can prove me wrong. —*Albert Einstein*

941 Destiny is not a matter of chance, it is a matter of choice, it is not a thing to be waited for, it is a thing to be achieved. —*W. J. Bryan*

942 Men are four:
He who knows not and knows not he knows not, he is a fool — shun him.
He who knows not and knows he knows not, he is simple — teach him.
He who knows and knows not he knows, he is asleep — wake him.
He who knows and knows he knows, he is wise — follow him!
—*Arabic Apothegm*

943 Reason is the life of the law; nay, the common law itself is nothing but reason. The law which is the perfection of reason.
—*Sir Edward Cokh*

944 Our knowledge is the amassed thought and experience of innumerable minds. —*Emerson*

945 Wisdom is only found in the truth. —*Goethe*

946 A man may die, nations may rise and fall, but an idea lives on. Ideas have endurance without death. —*John F. Kennedy*

947 Ken's Law: A flying particle will seek the nearest eye.

948 Schopenhauer's Law of Entropy: If you put a spoonful of wine in a barrel of sewage, you get sewage. If you put a spoonful of sewage in a barrel of wine, you get sewage.

949 Allen's Law: Almost anything is easier to get into than to get out of.

950 Young's Law of Inanimate Mobility: All inanimate objects can move just enough to get in your way.

951 Smith's Law: No real problem has a solution.

952 Baruch's Observation: If all you have is a hammer, everything looks like a nail.

953 And what is a weed? A plant whose virtues have not been discovered. —*Emerson*

954 Learn as if you were to live forever; live as if you were to die tomorrow.

955 He that scatters thorns, let him go barefoot.

956 Don't think to hunt two hares with one dog.

957 Many complain of their memory, few of their judgement.

958 Those who have nothing to trouble them, will surely be troubled by nothing.

959 The greatest conqueror is he who conquers himself.

960 In quietness and in confidence shall be your strength. —*Isaiah 30:15*

961 A good example is the best sermon.

962 Before you run in double harness, look well to the other horse.

963 A man must keep his mouth open a long, long while before a roast pigeon flies into it.

964 Old Serbian proverb: Don't run after women or trains, in ten minutes there will be another one.

965 Lack of planning on your part, does not constitute an emergency on my part.

966 Character is what you are in the dark. —*D. L. Moody*

RALPH WALDO EMERSON
American essayist and poet
May 25, 1803 - April 27, 1882

967 Books are embalmed minds. —*C. N. Bovee*

968 The early worm should read the proverbs.

969 Rather a magnificent defeat, than an ignoble victory.

970 He who trusts all things to chance makes a lottery of his life.

971 He that will not apply new remedies must expect new evils. —*Bacon*

972 Where the needle goes, the thread follows. —*Tolstoy*

973 The Russian has three strong principles: perhaps, somehow and never mind. —*Tolstoy*

974 If the rich could hire others to die for them, the poor could make a nice living.

975 We all have strength enough to endure the misfortunes of others. —*Francois de La Rochefoucauld*

976 Silence is the unbearable repartee. —*G. K. Chesterton*

977 Gluttony is an emotional escape, a sign that something is eating us. —*Peter De Vries*

978 Architecture is frozen music. —*Goethe*

979 Beauty is pleasure regarded as the quality of a thing. —*Santayana*

980 Out of thine own mouth will I judge thee. —*Luke 19:22*

981 Expect nothing and you will never be dissappointed.

982 In the fell clutch of circumstance, I have not winced nor cried aloud. Under the bludgeonings of chance my head is bloody, but unbowed. —*William Henley*

983 If I had eight hours to chop down a tree, I'd spend six sharpening my ax. —*Abraham Lincoln*

984 Unjust criticism is usually a disguised compliment. It often means that you have aroused jealousy and envy. Remember that no one ever kicks a dead dog. —*Dale Carnegie*

985 The art of life lies in a constant readjustment to our surroundings. —*Okakura Kakuzo*

986 Character is long-standing habit. —*Plutarch*

987 It is presence of mind in untried emergencies that the native metal of a man is tested. —*Lowell*

988 Coup de main. A sudden and unexpected movement or attack.

989 Silence is not always tact and it is tact that is golden, not silence. —*Samuel Butler*

990 The finest words in the world are only vain sounds if you cannot understand them. —*Anatole France*

991 Wit is the sudden marriage of ideas which before their marriage were not perceived to have any relation. —*Mark Twain*

992 Conditions are never just right. —*William Feather*

993 Success is getting what you want, happiness is wanting what you get. —*Charles F. Kettering*

994 Civilization is a limitless multiplication of unnecessary necessaries. —*Mark Twain*

995 An unattempted woman cannot boast of her chastity. —*Montaigne*

996   There is no bore like a clever bore. —*Samuel Butler*

997   The search for happiness is one of the chief sources of unhappiness.
—*Eric Hoffer*

998   As knowledge increases, wonder deepens. —*Charles Morgan*

999   To know and not to do is not yet to know. —*Zen proverb*

1000   I would rather see a crooked furrow than a field unplowed.
—*Paul Jewkes*

1001   There is no security on earth, there is only opportunity.
—*Douglas MacArthur*

1002   Man stays wise as long as he searches for wisdom, as soon as he thinks
he has found it, he becomes a fool. —*Talmud*

1003   He who is only wise lives a sad life. —*Voltaire*

1004   Let us never negotiate out of fear, but let us never fear to negotiate.
—*John F. Kennedy*

1005   What is more mortifying than to feel that you've missed the plum for
want of courage to shake the tree? —*Logan Smith*

1006   The wise man will build a hut on the ruins of his palace.
—*Russian proverb*

1007   Some fellows pay a compliment like they expected a receipt.
—*Kin Hubbard*

1008   *The signs of success are on the door. "Push" and "Pull".*
—*Yiddish proverb*

1009   Even a stopped clock is right twice a day. After some years it can boast
of a long series of successes. —*Ebner-Eschenbach*

1010   Forget injuries, never forget kindnesses —*Confucius*

NATHANIEL HAWTHORNE
American novelist
July 4, 1804 - May 19, 1864

1011 Education is the acquisition of the art of the utilization of knowledge. —*Alfred North Whitehead*

1012 To sow is less difficult than to reap. —*Goethe*

1013 It is a mistake to look too far ahead. Only one link in the chain of destiny can be handled at a time. —*Churchill*

1014 He who can endure all can dare all. —*Vauvennargues*

1015 Between two lawyers is like a fish between two cats. —*Benjamin Franklin*

1016 You can generally get success if you do not want victory. —*William Inge*

1017 The successes of the day belong to bold mediocrity. —*Ebner-Eschenbach*

1018 It is a mark of a good action that it appears inevitable in retrospect. —*Robert Louis Stevenson*

1019 He who lives without folly is hardly so wise as he thinks. —*La Rochefoucauld*

1020 We judge ourselves by what we feel capable of doing, while others judge us by what we have already done. —*Longfellow*

1021 A wise man knows everything; a shrewd one everybody.

1022 Did nothing in particular and did it very well. —*W. S. Gilbert*

1023 So much to do; so little done. —*Cecil Rhodes*

1024 He nothing common did, or mean, upon that memorable scene. —*Marvell*

1025 Adversity introduces a man to himself.

1026 Admonish your friends privately, but praise them openly. —*Syrus*

1027 A useless life is an early death. —*Goethe*

1028 A pound of pluck is worth a ton of luck. —*James A. Garfield*

1029 Adopt the pace of nature: her secret is patience. —*Emerson*

1030 A pessimist is one who feels bad when he feels good for fear he'll feel worse when he feels better.

1031 It is easier to catch flies with honey than with vinegar. —*English proverb*

1032 Principles become modified in practice by facts. —*Cooper*

1033 Error of opinion may be tolerated where reason is left free to combat it. —*Jefferson*

1034 No man ever yet became great by imitation. —*Samuel Johnson*

1035 Habits are at first cobwebs, then cables. —*Spanish proverb*

1036 The human race is governed by its imagination. —*Napoleon*

1037 You cannot make a crab walk straight. —*Aristophanes*

1038 An institution is the lengthened shadow of one man. —*Emerson*

1039 Inspiration and genius - one and the same. —*Victor Hugo*

1040 I take all knowledge to be my province. —*Bacon*

1041 One life — a little gleem of time between two eternities. —*Carlyle*

1042 Everybody is ignorant, only about different things. —*Will Rogers*

1043 It is better to be envied than pitied. —*Herodotus*

1044 Is there anyone so wise as to learn by the experience of others? —*Voltaire*

1045 An expert is a person who avoids the small errors as he sweeps on to the grand fallacy. —*Stolberg*

1046 Failure is more frequently from want of energy than want of capital. —*Daniel Webster*

1047 Faith is the force of life. —*Tolstoy*

1048 A sleeping fox counts hens in his dreams. —*Russian proverb*

1049 A gentleman is a man who can disagree without being disagreeable.

1050 No man's credit is as good as his money. —*E. W. Howe*

1051 We triumph without glory when we conquer without danger. —*Cornelle*

1052 Give me the ready hand rather than the ready tongue. —*Garibaldi*

1053 Disappointment is the nurse of wisdom. —*Sir Boyle Roche*

1054 The better part of valour is discretion. —*Shakespeare*

1055 Thou shouldst eat to live; not live to eat. —*Cicero*

1056 Hitch your wagon to a star. —*Emerson*

1057 Better to reign in hell than serve in heaven. —*Milton*

1058 If you wish to reach the highest, begin at the lowest. —*Syrus*

BENJAMIN DISRAELI
British statesman
December 21, 1804 - April 19, 1881

1059 Ah, to build, to build! That is the noblest of all the arts. —*Longfellow*

1060 If you always live with those who are lame, you will yourself learn to limp. —*Latin proverb*

1061 Little boats should keep near shore. —*Franklin*

1062 Common sense is very uncommon. —*Horace Greeley*

1063 When a dove begins to associate with crows its feathers remain white but its heart grows black. —*German proverb*

1064 I regret often that I have spoken; never that I have been silent. —*Syrus*

1065 The empty vessel makes the greatest sound. —*Shakespeare*

1066 A soft answer turneth away wrath. —*Proverbs 15:1*

1067 The mind grows by what it feeds on. —*J.G.Holland*

1068 Nine-tenths of wisdom consists in being wise in time. —*Theodore Roosevelt*

1069 If you cut off the head of a dog, the tail will die.

1070 The safest way to double your money is to fold it over once and put it in your pocket. —*Kin Hubbard*

1071 The author who speaks about his own books is almost as bad as a mother who talks about her own children. —*Disraeli*

1072 Mountains are earth's undecaying monuments. —*Hawthorne*

1073 Noblesse oblige, nobility obligates.

1074 Rather understated elegance, than overstated opulence.

1075   If truth were self-evident, eloquence would not be necessary. —*Cicero*

1076   Socrates thought that if all our misfortune were laid in one common heap, whence everyone must take an equal portion, most persons would be contented to take their own and depart.

1077   Living from hand to mouth. —*Du Bartas*

1078   Eloquence may set fire to reason. —*Oliver Wendell Holmes, Jr*

1079   Great flame follows a tiny spark. —*Dante*

1080   Hyt is not al gold that glareth. —*Chaucer*

1081   My wit is thynne. —*Chaucer*

1082   Be not angry that you cannot make others as you wish them to be, since you cannot make yourself as you wish to be. —*Thomas Kempis*

1083   It makes a difference whose ox is gored. —*Martin Luther*

1084   Let down the curtain the farce is done. —*Rabelais*

1085   Enough is as good as a feast. —*Heywood*

1086   Iron hand in a velvet glove. —*Charles V*

1087   Sits he on never so high a throne, a man still sits on his bottom. —*Montaigne*

1088   And swans seem whiter if swart crowes be by. —*Du Bartas*

1089   By a small sample we may judge of the whole piece. —*Cervantes*

1090   Nothing succeeds like success. —*Alexandre Dumas*

1091 All human wisdom is summed up in two words — wait and hope.
—*Alexandre Dumas*

1092 The reward of a thing well done, is to have done it. —*Emerson*

1093 I hate quotations. Tell me what you know. —*Emerson*

1094 Our chief want in life is somebody who shall make us do what we can.
—*Emerson*

1095 Dogmatism is puppyism come to its full growth. —*Jerrold*

1096 Little things affect little minds. —*Disraeli*

1097 The secret of success is constancy to purpose. —*Disraeli*

1098 Fate makes our relatives, choice makes our friends. —*Delille*

1099 We may affirm absolutely that nothing great in the world has been accomplished without passion. —*Hegel*

1100 One can acquire everything in solitude — except character. —*Beyle*

1101 The history of the world is but the biography of great men. —*Carlyle*

1102 All that mankind had done, thought, gained or been: it is lying as in magic preservation in the pages of books. —*Carlyle*

1103 *Be ashamed to die until you have won some victory for humanity.*
—*Horace Mann*

1104 The buyer needs a hundred eyes, the seller not one. —*George Herbert*

1105 Whatsoever a man soweth, that shall he also reap. —*Galatians 6:7*

1106 Obstinancy in a bad cause is but constancy in a good.
—*Sir Thomas Browne*

1107 Lack of money is the root of all evil. —*G. B. Shaw*

1108 Unlike my subject now shall be my song; it shall be witty, and it sha'n't be long. —*Chesterfield*

1109 It is better to live rich, than to die rich. —*Samuel Johnson*

1110 I am rich beyond the dreams of avarice. —*Edward Moore*

1111 The desire of knowledge, like the thirst of riches, increases ever with the acquisition of it. —*Lawrence Sterne*

1112 Which of you, intending to build a tower, sitteth not down first, and counteth the cost, whether he have sufficient to finish it? —*Luke 14:28*

1113 He that wants money, means, and content is without three good friends. —*Shakespeare*

1114 I do desire we may be better strangers. —*Shakespeare*

1115 Every man thinks his own geese swans. —*Dickens*

1116 Men's evil manners live in brass; their virtues we write in water. —*Shakespeare*

1117 True happiness consists not in the multitude of friends, but in the worth and choice. —*Ben Johnson*

1118 Or sells eternity to get a toy. —*Shakespeare*

1119 When he shall die, take him and cut him out in little stars. —*Shakespeare*

1120 The devil can cite Scripture for his purpose. —*Shakespeare*

1121 A hazard of new fortunes. —*Shakespeare*

1122 You may buy land now as cheap as stinking mackerel. —*Shakespeare*

1123 When we mean to build we first survey the plot, then draw the model; and when we see the figure of the house, then must we rate the cost of the erection. —*Shakespeare*

1124 A habitation giddy and unsure hath he that buildeth on the vulgar heart. —*Shakespeare*

1125 Like one that stands upon a promontory, and spies a far-off shore where he would tread, wishing his foot were equal with his eye. —*Shakespeare*

1126 Having nothing, nothing can he lose. —*Shakespeare*

1127 The eagle suffers little birds to sing. —*Shakespeare*

1128 No profit grows where is no pleasure ta'en; In brief, sir, study what you most affect. —*Shakespeare*

1129 And do as adversaries do in law, strive mightily, but eat and drink as friends. —*Shakespeare*

1130 The path is smooth that leadeth on to danger. —*Shakespeare*

1131 What matter if it be a fool's paradise? Paradise is paradise, for whoever owns it —*Peter Ibbetson*

1132 They are never alone that are accompanied with noble thoughts. —*Sir Philip Sidney*

1133 I will neither yield to the song of the siren nor the voice of the hyena the tears of the crocodile nor the howling of the wolf. —*George Chapman*

1134 Fortune is like the market, where many times, if you can stay a little, the price will fall. —*Francis Bacon*

GIUSEPPE GARIBALDI
Italian Nationalist leader
July 4, 1807 - June 2, 1882

1135 Glory is like a circle in the water, which never ceaseth to enlarge itself, till by broad spreading it disperse to nought. —*Shakespeare*

1136 I will make it a felony to drink small beer. —*Shakespeare*

1137 Fortune may have yet a better success in reserve for you, and they who lose today may win tomorrow. —*Cervantes*

1138 Every dog has his day. —*Cervantes*

1139 'Tis part of a wise man to keep himself today for tomorrow, and not venture all his eggs in one basket. —*Cervantes*

1140 Required in every good lover ... the whole alphabet ... agreeable, bountiful, constant, dutiful, easy, faithful, gallant, honourable, ingenious, kind, loyal, mild, noble, officious, prudent, quiet, rich, secret, true, valiant, wise, ... young, and zealous. —*Cervantes*

1141 Even a worm when trod upon, will turn again. —*Cervantes*

1142 Never look for birds of this year in the nests of the last. —*Cervantes*

1143 Any one can hold the helm when the sea is calm. —*P. Syrus*

1144 It is a bad plan that admits of no modification. —*P. Syrus*

1145 The best ideas are common property. —*Seneca*

1146 I was shipwrecked before I got aboard. —*Seneca*

1147 It has been related that dogs drink at the river Nile running along, that they may not be seized by the crocodiles. —*Phaedrus*

1148 Those who wish to appear wise among fools, among the wise seem foolish. —*Quintilian*

1149 Anacharsis coming to Athens, knocked at Solon's door, and told him that he, being a stranger, was come to be his guest, and contract a friendship with him; and Solon replied, "It is better to make friends at home," Anarcharsis replied, "Then you that are at home make friendship with me."

1150 Criticism comes easier than craftsmanship. —*Zeuxis*

1151 One swallow does not make a spring. —*Aristotle*

1152 In many ways the saying "Know thyself" is not well said. It were more practical to say "Know other people." —*Menander*

1153 There is no gathering the rose without being pricked by the thorns. —*Pilpay*

1154 Force without wisdom falls of its own weight. —*Horace*

1155 He has half the deed done, who has made a beginning. —*Horace*

1156 Even a single hair casts its shadow. —*P. Syrus*

1157 You should hammer your iron when it is glowing hot. —*P. Syrus*

1158 The first in banquets, but the last in fight. —*Homer*

1159 Character is destiny. —*Heraclitis*

1160 Men of perverse opinion do not know the excellence of what is in their hands, till some one dash it from them. —*Sophocles*

1161 To the fool, he who speaks wisdom will sound foolish. —*Euripides*

1162 Waste not fresh tears over old griefs. —*Euripides*

1163 Where two discourse, if the one's anger rise. The man who lets the contest fall is wise. —*Euripides*

1164 Every man is like the company he is wont to keep. —*Euripides*

1165 As a well-spent day brings happy sleep, so life well used brings happy death. —*Leonardo da Vinci*

1166 Nothing is so firmly believed as what we least know. —*Montaigne*

1167 If you seek a monument, look about you. —*Inscription on Sir Christopher Wren's tomb in St. Paul's Cathedral, London*

1168 If wishes were horses, beggers might ride. —*John Ray*

1169 It takes a wise man to know a wise man.

1170 A man convinced against his will is of the same opinion still.

1171 When in doubt punt. —*Knute Rockne*

1172 Money can't buy love, but it can put you in a very pleasant bargaining position.

1173 Those who complain about the way the ball bounces are often the ones who dropped it.

1174 May your bread always fall butter side up.

1175 It is of no consequence to be in a large town while you are reading. I read at New Salem, which never had three hundred people living in it. The books, and your capacity for understanding them are just the same in all places. —*A. Lincoln*

1176 Quid pro quo. Something for something.

1177 Gold is where you find it.

ABRAHAM LINCOLN
President of the United States, 1861-65
February 12, 1809 - April 15, 1865

1178 What went wrong: This is the story of four people, everybody, somebody, anybody and nobody.
There was an important job to be done and everybody was sure that somebody would do it.
Anybody could have done it, but nobody did it.
Somebody got angry because it was everybody's job.
Everybody thought that somebody would do it.
But nobody asked anybody.
It ended up that the job wasn't done and everybody blamed everybody, when actually nobody asked anybody.

1179 I was born when you kissed me, I died when you went away, and I lived the few weeks that you loved me.

1180 If you don't understand what you are getting into, then don't get into it.

1181 Little drops of water, little grains of sand, make the mighty ocean and the pleasant land. —*Julia Carney*

1182 My love boat is your gloat boat. —*Mike McKenna*

1183 A recession is when you live in the *lapse* of luxury.

1184 It is not necessary to blow out the other person's light just to let your own shine.

1185 When money is cheap, property is expensive; when property is cheap money is expensive.

1186 Temper is what gets most of us into trouble; pride is what keeps us there.

1187 Always bear in mind that your own resolution to succeed is more important than any other one thing. —*A. Lincoln*

1188 The more the marble wastes, the more the statue grows. —*Michelangelo*

1189 Let the streets be as wide as the height of the houses. —*Leonardo da Vinci*

1190 A smile costs nothing, but gives much. It enriches those who receive, without making poorer those who give. It takes but a moment, but the memory of it sometimes lasts forever. None is so rich or mighty that he can get along without it, and none is so poor but that he can be made rich by it. A smile creates happiness in the home, fosters good will in business, and is the countersign of friendship. It brings rest to the weary, cheer to the discouraged, sunshine to the sad, and it is nature's best antidote for trouble. Yet it cannot be bought, begged, borrowed, or stolen for it is something that is of no value to anyone until it is given away. Some people are too tired to give you a smile. Give them one of yours, as none needs a smile so much as he who has no more to give.

1191 It is more difficult to eliminate a preconceived judgement than it is to split an atom. —*Albert Einstein*

1192 Moderation in all things . . . except when you want success.

1193 Rome wasn't built in a day . . . but neither was Sodom and Gomorrah.

1194 Frank Lloyd Wright was called as a witness, for a jury trial, on a construction case. While being sworn in he was asked to state his name and occupation and stated, "Frank Lloyd Wright, the world's greatest architect." When he stepped down the attorney asked why he said this. His reply, "I was under oath."

1195 If you keep both feet on the ground all the time you wont get very far.

1196 Worry, the interest paid by those who borrow trouble. —*George Lyon*

1197 Gambrel roofs evolved from gable roofs, because they provided more useable space.

1198 Don't be a slave to your will power.

1199 A fanatic is a person who can't change his mind and wont change the subject.

1200 The odds on starting a task are greatly increased when you know exactly how to complete it.

1201 When the price is more than the value it is called, "a bad deal".

1202 If you have a $1,000 tax deduction, and are in a 30% tax bracket you have saved $300 on your taxes.

1203 I can resist everything except temptation. —*Oscar Wilde*

1204 What is a cynic? A man who knows the price of everything and the value of nothing. —*Oscar Wilde*

1205 Only in men's imagination does every truth find an effective and undeniable existence. Imagination, not invention is the supreme master of art as of life. —*Joseph Conrad*

1206 Genius, that power which dazzles mortal eyes, is oft but perseverance in disguise. —*Henry Austin*

1207 Only the game fish swims upstream. —*John Moore*

1208 Far better it is to dare mighty things, to win glorious triumphs, even though checkered by failure, than to take rank with those poor spirits who neither enjoy much nor suffer much, because they live in the gray twilight that knows not victory nor defeat. —*Theodore Roosevelt*

1209 The natural man has only two primal passions, to get and to beget. —*Sir William Osler*

1210 To be what we are, and to become what we are capable of becoming is the only end of life. —*Robert Louis Stevenson*

1211 My body, which my dungeon is, and yet my parks and palaces. —*Robert Louis Stevenson*

1212 A man travels the world over in search of what he needs and returns home to find it. —*George Moore*

ALFRED TENNYSON
English poet
August 6, 1809 - October 6, 1892

1213 Oh, was I born too soon, my dear, or were you born too late, That I am going out the door while you come in the gate? —*Henry Van Dyke*

1214 What this country needs is a good-five cent nickel. —*Franklin P. Adams*

1215 It is only one step from toleration to forgiveness. —*Walter Page*

1216 The ultimate tax shelter . . . no income.

1217 Life seems to me like a Japanese picture which our imagination does not allow to end with the margin. We aim at the infinite and when our arrow falls to earth it is in flames.
—*Justice Oliver Wendell Holmes, Jr.*

1218 To know is nothing at all, to imagine is everything. —*Anatole France*

1219 One does not know - cannot know - the best that is in one.
—*Nietzche*

1220 Architecture is a sort of oratory of power by means of forms.
—*Nietzche*

1221 Some are born posthumously. —*Nietzche*

1222 The wealth of mankind is the wisdom they leave. —*John O'Reilly*

1223 The sails we see on the ocean are as white as white can be; but never one in the harbor as white as the sails at sea. —*Charlotte Perry*

1224 Men are polished, through act and speech, each by each, as pebbles are smoothed on the rolling beach. —*Trowbridge*

1225 I hold that man is in the right who is most closely in league with the future. —*Henrik Ibsen*

1226 Let us all be happy and live within our means, even if we have to borrow the money to do it with. —*Charles Browne*

1227 A hen is only an egg's way of making another egg. —*Samuel Butler*

1228 Work consists of whatever a body is obliged to do ... play consists of whatever a body is not obliged to do. —*Mark Twain*

1229 You can not demonstrate an emotion or prove an aspiration. —*Viscount Morley*

1230 The great business of life is to be, to do, to do without, and to depart. —*Viscount Morley*

1231 A great city is that which has the greatest men and women. —*Whitman*

1232 Like a wave, which in no two consecutive moments of its existence is composed of the same particles. —*John Tyndall*

1233 Business? It's quite simple. It's other people's money. —*Alexandre Dumas*

1234 If a little knowledge is dangerous, where is the man who has so much as to be out of danger? —*Thomas Huxley*

1235 When the last individual of a race of living things breathes no more, another heaven and another earth must pass before such a one can be again. —*William Beebe*

1236 Trifles make the sum of life. —*Dickens*

1237 A man must take the fat with the lean. —*Dickens*

1238 The soil out of which such men as he are made is good to be born on, good to live on, good to die for and to be buried in. —*James R. Lowell*

1239 Waldo is one of those people who would be enormously improved by death —*Hector Munro*

1240 Win without boasting. Lose without excuse. —*Terhune*

1241 The significance of man is that he is insignificant and is aware of it.
—*Carl Becker*

1242 What's the use? Yesterday an egg, tomorrow a feather duster.
—*Fenderson*

1243 The world will never starve for wonders; but only for want of wonder.
—*Chesterton*

1244 There are some things which cannot be learned quickly, and time, which is all we have, must be paid heavily for their acquiring. They are the very simplest things and because it takes a man's life to know them the little new that each man gets from life is very costly and the only heritage he has to leave. —*Ernest Hemingway*

1245 We call Japanese soldiers fanatics when they die rather than surrender, wheras American soldiers who do the same thing are heroes. —*Robert Hutchins*

1246 His words leap across rivers and mountains, but his thoughts are still only six inches long. —*E. B. White*

1247 *You do not have to shout, but if you whisper ___ the whisper had better be good.* —*Robert Leavitt*

1248 The test of a first-rate intelligence is the ability to hold two opposed ideas in the mind at the same time, and still retain the ability to function. —*F. Scott Fitzgerald*

1249 I had to sink my yacht to make the guests go home.
—*F. Scott Fitzgerald*

1250 Pessimism is only the name that men of weak nerves give to wisdom.
—*Mark Twain*

1251 I decline to accept the end of man . . . I believe that man will not merely endure: he will prevail. —*William Faulkner*

1252 There could be no honour in a sure success, but much might he wrested from a sure defeat. —*T. E. Lawrence*

1253 He couldn't design a cathedral without it looking like the First Supernatural Bank! —*Eugene O'Neill*

1254 Alexandre Dumas when asked how he had enjoyed a dull party replied, "I should not have enjoyed it if I had not been there."

1255 There's only one corner of the universe you can be certain of improving, and that's your own self. —*Aldous Huxley*

1256 I am a member of the rabble in good standing. —*Westbrook Pegler*

1257 Well, if I called the wrong number, why did you answer the phone? —*James Thurber*

1258 He plows the sand at his hardest need, he sows himself for seed. —*Elinor Wylie*

1259 He whom a dream hath possessed knoweth no more of doubting. —*Shaemas O'Sheel*

1260 Ed Wynn explaining why he sold his farm: Every raddish I ever pulled up seemed to have a mortgage attached to it.

1261 Diplomacy is to do and say the nastiest things in the nicest way. —*Isaac Goldberg*

1262 There is less in this than meets the eye. —*Alexander Wollcott*

1263 I'd rather have an inch of dog than miles of pedigree. —*Dana Burnet*

1264 When the One Great Scorer comes to write against your name — He marks — not that you won or lost — but how you played the game. —*Grantland Rice*

1265 If you couldn't afford good whisky, he'd take you on trust for beer. —*Gerald Brennan*

1266 You must keep your goal in sight, labor toward it day and night, then at last arriving there, you shall be too old to care. —*Witter Bynner*

1267 The world would sleep if things were run, by men who say, "It can't be done." —*P. Johnson*

1268 Saddle your dreams afore you ride 'em. —*Mary Webb*

1269 If not actually disgruntled, he was far from being gruntled. —*Wodehouse*

1270 With doubt and dismay you are smitten, you think there's no chance for you son? Why, the best books haven't been written. The best race hasn't been run. —*Berton Braley*

1271 It is even possible that laws which have not their origin in the mind may be irrational, and we can never succeed in formulating them. —*Sir Arthur Eddington*

1272 Hit hard, hit fast, hit often. —*Admiral Halsey*

1273 It is common sense to take a method and try it: If it fails, admit it frankly and try another. But above all, try something. —*Franklin D. Roosevelt*

1274 I have learned silence from the talkative, toleration, from the intolerant, and kindness from the unkind; yet strange, I am ungrateful to those teachers. —*Kahlil Gibran*

1275 Words ought to be a little wild for they are the assault of thoughts on the unthinking. —*Lord Keynes*

1276 There are two cardinal sins from which all others spring; impatience and laziness. —*Franz Kafka*

OLIVER WENDELL HOLMES
American poet and physician
August 29, 1809 - October 7, 1894

1277 I am the captain of my soul; I rule it with stern joy; and yet I think I had more fun when I was a cabin boy. —*Keith Preston*

1278 Men do not understand books until they have had a certain amount of life, or at any rate no man understands a deep book, until he has seen and lived at least a part of its contents. —*Ezra Pound*

1279 Avoid the reeking herd, shun the polluted flock, live like that stoic bird the eagle of the rock. —*Elinor Wylie*

1280 I consider your conduct unethical and lousy. —*Peter Arno*

1281 Ennui, felt on the proper occasions, is a sign of intelligence. —*Clifton Fadiman*

1282 If you give to a thief he cannot steal from you, and he is then no longer a thief. —*William Saroyan*

1283 Oh wad some power the giftie gie us, to see oursels as others see us. —*Robert Burns*

1284 God knows, I'm no the thing I should be, nor am I even the thing I could be. —*Robert Burns*

1285 Making the world safe for hypocrisy. —*Thomas Wolfe*

1286 Woman's virtue is man's greatest invention. —*Cornelia Otis Skinner*

1287 I think that I shall never see a billboard lovely as a tree, indeed, unless the billboards fall I'll never see a tree at all. —*Ogden Nash*

1288 Middle age is when you've met so many people that every new person you meet reminds you of someone else. —*Ogden Nash*

1289 I believe a little incompatibility is the spice of life, particularly if he has income and she is pattable. —*Ogden Nash*

1290 A sophistical rhetorician, inebriated with the exuberance of his own verbosity —*Disraeli*

1291 Speech is the index of the mind. —*Seneca*

1292 There are three marks of a superior man: being virtuous, he is free from anxiety; being wise, he is free from perplexity; being brave, he is free from fear. —*Confucius*

1293 *My tastes are aristocratic; my actions democratic.* —*Victor Hugo*

1294 The mind grows by what it feeds on. —*J. G. Holland*

1295 Time is money. —*Bulwer-Lytton*

1296 Better to wear out than to rust out. —*Bishop Cumberland*

1297 Think much, speak little, and write less. —*Italian proverb*

1298 That which is striking and beautiful is not always good; but that which is good is always beautiful. —*Ninon de L'Enclos*

1299 Knowledge is proud that he has learn'd so much; wisdom is humble that he knows no more. —*Cowper*

1300 We give advice by the bucket, but take it by the grain —*W. R. Alger*

1301 He who will not answer to the rudder, must answer to the rocks. —*Herve*

1302 Antiquity cannot privilege an error, nor novelty prejudice a truth.

1303 If I shoot at the sun I may hit a star. —*P. T. Barnum*

1304 They make glorious shipwreck who are lost in seeking worlds. —*Lessing*

1305 The mere aspiration is partial realization —*Anna Cora Mowatt*

1306 Lord, grant that I may always desire more than I can accomplish. —*Michelangelo*

1307 Property is at once the consequence and the basis of the state. —*Baklinin*

1308 I can tell where my own shoe pinches me. —*Cervantes*

1309 Imitation is the sincerest form of flattery. —*Colton*

1310 The mill cannot grind with water that has past. —*Sarah Doudney*

1311 Silence gives consent. —*Thomas Fuller*

1312 Wouldst thou both eat thy cake and have it? —*Herbert*

1313 That was laid on with a trowel. —*Shakespeare*

1314 Cut off your nose to spite your face. —*des Reaux*

1315 He is a self-made man, and worships his creator. —*John Bright*

1316 No one is exempt from talking nonsense; the misfortune is to do it solemnly. —*Montaigne*

1317 An optimist sees an opportunity in every calamity; a pessimist sees a calamity in every opportunity.

1318 Keep your face to the sunshine and you cannot see the shadow. —*Helen Keller*

1319 He was a bold man that first ate an oyster. —*Swift*

1320 In fair weather prepare for foul. —*Thomas Fuller*

ROBERT BROWNING
English Poet
May 7, 1812 - December 12, 1889

1321 He who is the most slow in making a promise is the most faithful in the performance of it. —*Rousseau*

1322 People seldom improve when they have no other model but themselves to copy after. —*Goldsmith*

1323 Men learn while they teach. —*Seneca*

1324 From listening comes wisdom, and from speaking repentance. —*Italian proverb*

1325 What is mind? No matter. What is matter? Never mind. —*T. H. Key*

1326 The wise man sees in the misfortunes of others what he should avoid. —*Syrus*

1327 Man is the only animal that blushes, or needs to. —*Mark Twain*

1328 When money speaks the truth is silent. —*Russian proverb*

1329 An army of stags led by a lion would be better than an army of lions led by a stag. —*Latin proverb*

1330 If the blind lead the blind, both shall fall into the ditch. —*Matthew 15:14*

1331 The pen is the tongue of the mind. —*Cervantes*

1332 All the known world, excepting only savage nations, is governed by books. —*Voltaire*

1333 Bore: a person who talks when you wish him to listen. —*Bierce*

1334 No army can withstand the strength of an idea whose time has come. —*Victor Hugo*

1335 There are three ingredients in the good life: learning, earning, and yearning. —*Christopher Morley*

1336 The ant finds kingdoms in a foot of ground. —*Benet*

1337 The future is something which everyone reaches at the rate of sixty minutes an hour, whatever he does, whoever he is. —*Clive Lewis*

1338 There is a certain blend of courage, integrity, character and principle which has no satisfactory dictionary name but has been called different things in different countries at different times. Our American name for it is "guts". —*Louis Adamic*

1339 Perhaps the exhaustion of the passions is the beginning of wisdom. —*James Hilton*

1340 In war: resolution. In defeat: defiance. In victory: magnanimity. In peace: good will. —*Churchill*

1341 The vagabond, when rich, is called a tourist. —*Paul Richard*

1342 A promise made is a debt unpaid. —*Robert Service*

1343 We can only pay our debt to the past by putting the future in debt to ourselves —*John Buchan*

1344 Order and simplification are the first steps toward the mastery of a subject — the actual enemy is the unknown. —*Thomas Mann*

1345 We should all be concerned about the future because we will have to spend the rest of our lives there. —*Charles Kettering*

1346 An idea isn't responsible for the people who believe in it. —*Donald Marquis*

1347 The universe is not hostile, nor yet is it friendly, it is simply indifferent. —*John Holmes*

1348 He has achieved success who has lived well, laughed often and loved much. —*Bessie Stanley*

1349 It is true art to conceal art.

1350 If you call a tail a leg, how many legs has a dog? Five? No, calling a tail a leg don't make it a leg. —*Lincoln*

1351 'Tis better to have loved and lost than never to have loved at all. —*Tennyson*

1352 A man is as big as the things that make him mad . . . that makes me a midget.

1353 For manners are not idle, but the fruit of loyal nature and of noble mind. —*Tennyson*

1354 There's a sucker born every minute. —*P. T. Barnum*

1355 Well-timed silence hath more eloquence than speech. —*Tupper*

1356 Faultless to a fault. —*Browning*

1357 There is a certain satisfaction in feeling you are bearing with heroic resignation the irritating folly of others. —*Jerome Jerome*

1358 There are two ways of spreading light: to be the candle or the mirror that reflects it. —*Edith Wharton*

1359 Though I've belted you an' flayed you, by the livin' Gawd that made you, you're a better man than I am, Gunga Din! —*Kipling*

1360 There is no limit to what you can accomplish, as long as you do not care who gets the credit.

1361 Money of last resort. Have a money-belt filled with gold and silver coins, secured in a safe deposit box at, or near, an airport. If anarchy arrives you leave all behind, put on your money-belt, and fly to a more stable destination.

1362 Every once in a while you have to look at the board and maybe you have to knock your king over and concede. But then you just set up the pieces and start over. —*Nolan Bushnell*

1363 The guardians of the valley of truth are chaos and confusion.

1364 The stars as you see them tonight never existed. —*Sir Arthur Eddington*

1365 Consider our star, the Sun, which is the only one of 200 billion other stars in the Milky Way galaxy. The universe contains at least 100 billion other galaxies. Each galaxy having at least 100 billion stars.

1366 On our planet earth we are both guest and prisoner.

1367 The light you see coming from the center of the Milky Way left there 30,000 years ago.

1368 Do something in the present to benefit the future.

1369 AIDAS. Attention, interest, desire, action, satisfaction. The steps in the sales process.

1370 You can't teach an old (or a very dumb) dog new tricks ... without first getting his attention.

1371 Fish or cut bait.

1372 From a letter written to a distributor who violated an exclusive contract: All you have done is confuse the customer and antagonize us.

1373 Education is going from the known to the unknown.
—*Major Robert Saunders*

1374 Better the power of love, than the love of power.

1375 Even God cannot change the past. —*Agathon*

1376 A plausible impossibility is always preferable to an unconvincing possibility. —*Aristotle*

1377 A wise man will make more opportunities than he finds. —*Francis Bacon*

1378 All generalizations are dangerous, even this one. —*Alexandre Dumas*

1379 We boil at different degrees. —*Emerson*

1380 He that lives upon hope will die fasting. —*Franklin*

1381 In two words: im-possible. —*Samuel Goldwyn*

1382 Love is the wisdom of the fool and the folly of the wise. —*Dr. Samuel Johnson*

1383 Genius does what it must, and talent does what it can. —*Owen Meredith*

1384 The worth of a state, in the long run, is the worth of the individuals composing it. —*John Stuart Mill*

1385 The greatest thing in the world is to know how to be self-sufficient. —*Montaigne*

1386 If triangles invented a god, they would make him three-sided. —*Montesquieu*

1387 From the sublime to the ridiculous there is only one step. —*Napoleon Bonaparte*

1388 Don't clap too hard — it's a very old building. —*John Osborne*

1389 The more intelligence one has the more people one finds original. Commonplace people see no difference between men. —*Blaise Pascal*

HENRY DAVID THOREAU
American naturalist and author
July 12, 1817 - May 6, 1862

1390 Success is the realization of the estimate which you place upon yourself. —*Elbert Hubbard*

1391 Success is that old ABC - ability, breaks, and courage. —*Charles Luckman*

1392 The art of living is more like wrestling than of dancing; the main thing is to stand firm and be ready for an unforseen attack. —*Marcus Aurelius*

1393 The man who makes no mistakes does not usually make anything. —*E. J. Phelps*

1394 Work banishes those three great evils: boredom, vice and poverty. —*Voltaire*

1395 Happiness is no laughing matter. —*Archbishop Whately*

1396 Then, sir, you will turn it over once more in what you are pleased to call your mind. —*Lord Westbury*

1397 A vacation is what you take when you can no longer take what you've been taking. —*Earl Wilson*

1398 Where all think alike, no one thinks very much. —*Walter Lippmann*

1399 Good architecture lets nature in. —*I. M. Pei*

1400 It should be possible to explain the laws of physics to a barmaid. —*Albert Einstein*

1401 We must have respect for both our plumbers and our philosophers or neither our pipes or our theories will hold water. —*John Gardner*

1402 Experience is not what happens to a man. It is what a man does with what happens to him. —*Aldous Huxley*

1403 Civilization begins with order, grows with liberty, and dies with chaos. —*Will Durant*

1404 You have not done enough, you have never done enough, so long as it is possible that you have something of value to contribute. —*Dag Hammarskjold*

1405 I'm lonesome. They are all dying. I have hardly a warm personal enemy left. —*J. A. Whistler*

1406 The man who can dominate a London dinner-table can dominate the world. —*Oscar Wilde*

1407 The great use of life is to spend it for something that outlasts it. —*William James*

1408 Success is self-expressionism at a profit. —*Marcelene Cox*

1409 Success is finding unobjectionable means for individual self-assertion. —*Eric Hoffer*

1410 The dictionary is the only place where success comes before work. —*Arthur Brisbane*

1411 Success is just a matter of luck. Ask any failure. —*Earl Wilson*

1412 Take care to get what you like or you will be forced to like what you get. —*Bernard Shaw*

1413 If you can count your money, you dont have a billion dollars. —*J. Paul Getty*

1414 Try not to become a man of success but rather try to become a man of value. —*Albert Einstein*

1415 To pull yourself up by your own bootstraps, shoulder to the wheel, and nose to the grindstone . . . can be uncomfortable

1416 The end of civilization is only 72 hours away. That is how long it takes before a starving man eats his dog.

1417 The'll have your guts for garters

1418 The group of nobel laureates was one of the most intelligent gatherings ever ... with the possible exception of when Albert Einstein dined alone.

1419 You can't make love when you are in two different rooms.

1420 Oh, what a tangled web we weave when first we practise to deceive. —*Sir Walter Scott*

1421 In a private meeting with the founder of AMPEX, I asked how he selected that name. He replied, he put "excellence" after his own name: A. M. Poniatoff

1422 The quality of a person's life is in direct proportion to their commitment to excellence, regardless of their chosen field of endeavor. —*Vincent T. Lombardi*

1423 Better to remain silent and be thought a fool than to speak out and remove all doubt. —*Abraham Lincoln*

1424 It is a funny thing about life; if you refuse to accept anything but the best you very often get it. —*Somerset Maugham*

1425 Don't be humble; you're not that great. —*Golda Meir*

1426 As said to a person constantly complaining of what you write: Where were you when the page was blank?

1427 Once burned twice shy.

1428 POSH. Wealthy Englishmen traveling by ship from India to England did not want the heat of the sun in their cabin, and requested: Port Out, Starboard Home.

1429   If we steal thoughts from the moderns, it will be cried down as plagiarism; if from the ancients, it will be cried up as erudition. —*Colton*

1430   Men do less than they ought unless they do all that they can. —*Carlyle*

1431   He is all style and no class.

1432   An increase in anarchy, increases the price of gold, and lowers the value of property. —*R. T. M.*

1433   Gangplank mentality. I have mine. I am on board pull up the gangplank.

1434   Every architectural masterpiece begins with the sewer.

1435   It's a little tough ruling the world from the bottom.

1436   I hope this book will age like a good wine, and be more enjoyable as it grows older.

1437   Would you play Russian roulette for a million dollars? I hope not.

1438   Mr Bernard Shaw has no enemies but is intensely disliked by all his friends. —*Oscar Wilde*

1439   Chaos occurs when human rights are not respected. —*Andrew Young*

1440   What you see is what you get, and what you saw is all there ever was. —*R. T. M.*

1441   I hear that melting pot stuff a lot, and all I can say is that we haven't melted. —*Jessie Jackson*

1442   It is the ear that troubles the mouth. —*Ghana proverb*

1443 No one tests the depth of a river with both his feet.
—*Ivory Coast proverb*

1444 Never try to catch a black cat at night. —*Liberian proverb*

1445 If you wait for tomorrow, tomorrow comes. If you don't wait for tomorrow, tomorrow comes. —*Ivory Coast proverb*

1446 That's the worst of erudition — that the next scholar sucks the few drops of honey that you have accumulated, sets right your blunders, and you are superseded. —*A. C. Benson*

1447 One could say that the courage to be is the courage to accept oneself as accepted in spite of being unacceptable. —*Paul Tillich*

1448 First learn to love yourself, and then you can love me.
—*Saint Bernard of Clairvaux*

1449 If you do not believe in yourself, do not blame others for lacking faith in you. —*Brendon Francis*

1450 Work out your own salvation. Do not depend on others. —*Buddha*

1451 Everyone is wise until he speaks. —*Irish proverb*

1452 The art of being wise is the art of knowing what to overlook.
—*William James*

1453 A wise man among the ignorant is as a beautiful girl in the company of blind men. —*Saadi*

1454 The attempt to combine wisdom and power has only rarely been successful and then only for a short while. —*Albert Einstein*

1455 Growth in wisdom may be exactly measured by decrease in bitterness.
—*Nietzsche*

HENRIK IBSEN
Norwegian dramatist
March 20, 1828 - May 23, 1906

1456 Cleverness and stupidity are generally in the same boat against wisdom. —*J. A. Spender*

1457 It is only by risking our persons from one hour to the another that we live at all. —*William James*

1458 As useless as a blind man turning around to look. —*Nigerian proverb*

1459 A man's deeds are his life —*Ibo proverb*

1460 Hail Caesar, we who are about to die salute you.
—*Salutation of gladiators entering the arena*

1461 No one is without knowledge except he who asks no questions.
—*Cameroon proverb*

1462 Property is the prop of life. —*Chad proverb*

1463 However far the stream flows it never forgets its source.
—*Dahomey proverb*

1464 The teeth serve as a fence to the mouth. —*Gambia proverb*

1465 Poverty without debt is real wealth. —*Egyptian proverb*

1466 Don't be afraid to take a big step when one is indicated. You can't cross a chasm in two small jumps. —*David Lloyd George*

1467 Don't ever slam the door; you might want to go back. —*Don Herold*

1468 The best way to keep good acts in memory is to replenish them with new. —*Cato*

1469 Never argue; repeat your assertion. —*Robert Owen*

1470 Beware of a man of one book. —*English proverb*

1471 Don't think there are no crocodiles because the water is calm.
—*Malayan proverb*

1472 If you would be remembered do one thing superbly well.
—*Saunders Norvell*

1473 Measure a thousand times and cut once. —*Turkish proverb*

1474 Fall seven times, stand up eight. —*Japanese proverb*

1475 Do not fear death so much, but rather the inadequate life.
—*Bertolt Brecht*

1476 Hit the ball over the fence and you can take your time going around the bases. —*John W. Raper*

1477 Don't fall before you're pushed. —*English proverb*

1478 To know the road ahead, ask those coming back. —*Chinese proverb*

1479 Every vein affects the heart. —*Haitian proverb*

1480 Let him who wishes to hatch sit on his own eggs. —*Haitian proverb*

1481 Don't chain your dog with sausages.

1482 If you start to take Vienna—take Vienna. —*Napoleon*

1483 Get action. Do things; be sane, don't fritter away your time ... take a place wherever you are and be somebody; get action.
—*Theodore Roosevelt*

1484 It is not enough to aim; you must hit. —*Italian proverb*

1485 He who would leap high must take a long run. —*Danish proverb*

1486 The reason why worry kills more people than work is that more people worry than work. —*Robert Frost*

1487 The secret of walking on water, is knowing where the rocks are.

1488 I got what it takes—but it breaks my heart to give it away.

1489 The winds and waves are always on the side of the ablest navigators. —*Gibbon*

1490 As to business: Ready, fire, aim. —*Tom Peters*

1491 Consider well what your strength is equal to, and what exceeds your ability. —*Horace*

1492 An able man shows his spirit by gentle words and resolute actions. —*Chesterfield*

1493 The art of using moderate abilities to advantage wins praise, and often acquires more reputation than actual brilliancy. —*La Rochefoucauld*

1494 Men, like bullets go furthest when they are smoothest. —*Jean Paul Richter*

1495 The wicked are always surprised to find ability in the good. —*Vauvenargues*

1496 Jamais vu. The reverse of deja vu. You have never seen before.

1497 Some men see things as they are and say, why. I dream things that never were and say why not. —*Robert Kennedy*

1498 The dawn of knowledge is usually the false dawn. —*Bernard de Voto*

1499 Each honest calling, each walk of life, has its own elite, its own aristocracy based on excellence of performance. —*James B. Conant*

1500 Don't buy fresh strawberries in January.

1501 You can only see what you are looking for.

1502 CTSP (CATSUP). The Rules of Rot acronym: clever, true, short, positive.

1503 You don't have to teach a prostitute how to pull up her skirt.
—*Vietnamese proverb*

1504 If your outgo exceeds your income. Your upkeep will be your downfall.

1505 Deep down he is shallow.

1506 In Hollywood once you get beyond the tinsel, you get to the real tinsel.

1507 80% of life is showing up. —*Woody Allen*

1508 Nothing is more terrible than to see ignorance in action. —*Goethe*

1509 He who goes in circles shall someday be a big wheel.

1510 Act well at the moment, and you will have performed a good action to all eternity. —*Lavater*

1511 It's hard to be nice with a negative cash flow.

1512 The psychological version of the Golden Rule: People do unto others as they perceive others have done unto them.

1513 I pride myself in recognizing and upholding ability in every party and wherever I meet it. —*Beaconsfield*

1514 Who does the best his circumstance allows, does well, acts nobly; angels could do no more. —*Young*

1515 In abundance prepare for scarcity. —*Mencius*

1516 Our best thought comes from others. —*Emerson*

1517 The merely well-informed man is the most useless bore on God's earth. —*Alfred North Whitehead*

1518 Truth has no special time of its own. Its hour is now—always. —*Albert Schweitzer*

1519 All of our ideas come from the natural world: trees equal umbrellas. —*Wallace Stevens*

1520 One of the best ways to persuade others is with your ears — by listening to them. —*Dean Rusk*

1521 Goethe said there would be little left of him if he were to discard what he owed to others.

1522 There is nothing original; all is reflected light. —*Balzac*

1523 The type in all the books ever printed is either serif or sans serif.

1524 Birth, life, death, infinity.

1525 Gloat quote, quote gloat.

1526 This book could give plagiarism a good name.

1527 A high order of a low craft.

1528 Iterative enhancement. Adding to existing.

1529 The only thing that will redeem mankind is cooperation. —*Bertrand Russell*

1530 The whole of science is nothing more than a refinement of everyday thinking. —*Albert Einstein*

ANATOLE FRANCE
French novelist
April 16, 1844 - October 13, 1924

1531 Every man has to seek in his own way to make his own self more noble and realize his own true worth. —*Albert Schweitzer*

1532 We can't cross a bridge until we come to it; but I always like to lay down a pontoon ahead of time. —*Bernard Baruch*

1533 Your own home can be world headquarters for thinking.

1534 He who rises earliest sees the sun at its brightest, and reaps first the day's rewards.

1535 Ask not how you will fill your days left on earth, but how full you have made the days you have been given.

1536 THINK. —*Motto of IBM*

1537 If you find it boring to be with yourself, think what it must be for people that join you.

1538 The beauty is still on duty.

1539 If you can't enjoy life, hope for a happy death.

1540 The trouble with our age is all signpost and no destination. —*Louis Kronenberger*

1541 To find out what one is fitted to do and to secure an opportunity to do it is the key to happiness. —*John Dewey*

1542 When a man sits with a pretty girl for an hour, it seems like a minute. But let him sit on a hot stove for a minute — and it's longer than any hour. That's relativity. —*Albert Einstein*

1543 Duty, honor, country. —*Motto of West Point*

1544 No pain, no gain.

1545 Socrates had a favorite question: Why?

1546 Go ahead — Make my day. —*Ronald Reagan*

1547 Asking my banker for a loan, is like asking Bernhard Goetz for $5 on the subway.

1548 Nobody can eat a whole loaf of bread. Anybody can eat one slice at a time.

1549 Happiness makes up in height for what it lacks in length. —*Robert Frost*

1550 It is easier to love humanity as a whole than to love one's neighbor. —*Eric Hoffer*

1551 Horse sense is what a horse has that keeps him from betting on people. —*W. C. Fields*

1552 Baloney is the unvarnished lie laid on so thick you hate it. Blarney is flattery laid on so thin you love it. —*Fulton Sheen*

1553 A parrot can speak the words of Plato.

1554 If you think of each subject as a color; your life is a rainbow.

1555 People get defensive when they are attacked.

1556 Don't make a fetish of your eccentricities.

1557 There was a time I spoke in rhyme. Now I gloat and speak in quote. —*R. T. M.*

1558 Any outfit in the world has at least 10% waste. You're wasting your time listening to me. —*J. Peter Grace*

1559 Action may not always bring happiness; but there is no happiness without action. —*Beaconsfield*

1560 Never give in! Never give in! Never, never, never, never, — in nothing great or small, large or petty — never give in except to convictions of honor and good sense. —*Winston Churchill*

1561 The question, "Who ought to be boss?" is like asking "Who ought to be the tenor in the quartet?" Obviously, the man who can sing tenor. —*Henry Ford*

1562 If discretion is the better part of valor ... I am probably indiscreet.

1563 Rather than spend $5,000 on a machine, better to first spend $100 on a course explaining it.

1564 Action is eloquence, and the eyes of the ignorant are more learned than their ears. —*Shakespeare*

1565 In order to make an interpretation that a person will accept. It must be close enough to what they already believe, but also far enough away to make it worth saying.

1566 When a man points a finger at someone else, he should remember that four of his fingers are pointing at himself. —*Louis Nizer*

1567 The pursuit of truth shall set you free — even if you never catch up with it. —*Clarence Darrow*

1568 To be able to fill leisure intelligently is the last product of civilization. —*Bertrand Russell*

1569 One-liners can take a lifetime to accomplish.

1570 Prejudice, or wisdom, enable a person to make up their mind when they have insufficient information. Prejudice is a cheap substitution for wisdom.

1571 Reading between the lines of this book you will find only white paper.

1572 Our perceptions get in the way of our learning.

1573 Tons of words for a nugget of wisdom.

1574 Burn your candle at one end.

1575 Wit is skewed wisdom. Wisdom is sculpted foolishness. —*R. T. M.*

1576 More men are killed by overwork than the importance of the world justifies. —*Rudyard Kipling*

1577 We write our own destiny . . . we become what we do. —*Madame Chiang Kai-shek*

1578 A general definition of civilization: a civilized society is exhibiting the fine qualities of truth, beauty, adventure, art, peace. —*Alfred North Whitehead*

1579 Give wind and tide a chance to change. —*Richard E. Byrd*

1580 Brevity is the soul of wit. —*Shakespeare*

1581 What is the difference between license and sentence? License is permission to do what you want to do. A sentence is coercion to do what you do not want to do.
    An obligation without coercion is not a sentence.

1582 If something is too huge it isn't a pleasure, it is inventory.

1583 God answers all prayers — if we are silent enough to hear His reply.

1584 Drink not wine by the barrell, sip thy draft to thy thirst.

1585 Only he who would conquer, dares to fly above the eagles.
—*William the Conqueror*

1586 It is an insult to say that knowledge is worth its weight in gold.

1587 Comprehension is easy; absorption is difficult.

1588 It is conceivable that taking any subject and breaking it into one-liners is a new art form.

1589 I'm smarter than I look.

1590 Marcel Duchamp selected a shovel and hung it on a gallery wall. He maintained that his selection was the art.

1591 There's something disturbing about stupidity made coherent.

1592 I beg your pardon. I resemble that remark.

1593 My tongue has an I. Q. of 190. —*Nemen Coury*

1594 I'm chewing pennies.

1595 Take the pick of the litter.

1596 His conceit, is my self-confidence.

1597 It has always seemed to me that the most difficult part of building a bridge would be the start. —*Robert Benchley*

1598 The world today doesn't make sense, so why should I paint pictures that do? —*Pablo Picasso*

1599 I believe in the forgiveness of sin and the redemption of ignorance.
—*Adlai Stevenson*

SIR WILLIAM OSLER
Canadian physician
July 12, 1849 - December 29, 1919

1600 I've been rich and I've been poor; rich is better. —*Sophie Tucker*

1601 The most incomprehensible thing about the world is that it is comprehensible. —*Albert Einstein*

1602 He speaks through the flowers. —*German saying*

1603 He could teach an elephant to skip-rope.

1604 Better than a sharp stick in the eye.

1605 When we cannot act as we wish, we must act as we can. —*Terrence*

1606 The one sole determinate of success is our hidden self-esteem. —*Dr. Maxwell Maltz*

1607 A great person is an ordinary person with an extraordinary amount of determination. —*Dan Gable, U. S. Olympic wrestling coach*

1608 Anticipate the difficult by managing the easy. —*Lao-Tze*

1609 Collect as pearls the words of the wise and virtuous. —*Abd-el-Kader*

1610 Aphorisms are portable wisdom, the quintessential extracts of thought and feeling. —*W. R. Alger*

1611 The bigot's mind is like the pupil of the eye, - the more light you let into it the more it contracts. —*O. W. Holmes*

1612 He may justly be numbered among the benefactors of mankind who contracts the great rules of life into short sentences, that they may be easily impressed on the memory, and taught by frequent recollection to recur habitually to the mind. —*Johnson*

1613 Apothegms are the most infallible mirror to represent a man truly for what he is. —*Plutarch*

1614 A miser grows rich by seeming poor; an extravagant man grows poor by seeming rich. —*Shenstone*

1615 Behavior is a mirror in which everyone shows his image. —*Goethe*

1616 She looks as if butter wouldn't melt in her mouth. —*Swift*

1617 That gloomy outside, like a rusty chest, contains the shining treasure of a soul resolved and brave. —*Dryden*

1618 By appreciation we make excellence in others our own property. —*Voltaire*

1619 What is art? Nature concentrated. —*Balzac*

1620 No man can ever rise above that at which he aims. —*Rev. A. A. Hodge*

1621 Assertion, unsupported by fact, is nugatory; surmise and general abuse, in however elegant language, ought not to pass for proofs. —*Junius*

1622 He that walketh with wise men shall be wise. —*Solomon*

1623 No man can possibly improve in any company for which he has not respect enough to be under some degree of restraint. —*Chesterfield*

1624 It is a way of calling a man a fool when no attention is given to what he says. —*L'Estrange*

1625 Her frowns are fairer far than smiles of other maidens are. —*Coleridge*

1626 Avarice is only prudence and economy pushed to excess. —*Chatfield*

1627 What a spendthrift he is of his tongue. —*Shakespeare*

1628 When I said I would die a bachelor, I did not think I should live till I were married. —*Shakespeare*

1629 Whatever begins, also ends. —*Seneca*

1630 He that will believe only what he can fully comprehend, must have a very long head, or a very short creed. —*C. C. Colton*

1631 Carve your name on hearts, and not on marble. —*Spurgeon*

1632 When my friends are one-eyed, I look at their profile. —*Joubert*

1633 He who waits to do a great deal of good at once, will never do anything. —*Samuel Johnson*

1634 One anecdote of a man is worth a volume of biography. —*Channing*

1635 Who falls from all he knows of bliss, cares little into what abyss. —*Byron*

1636 The smaller the calibre of mind, the greater the bore of a perpetually open mouth. —*O. W. Holmes*

1637 Borrowing from Peter to pay Paul. —*Cicero*

1638 That's a valiant flea that does eat his breakfast on the lip of a lion. —*Shakespeare*

1639 No man can be brave who thinks pain the greatest evil; nor temperate, who considers pleasure the highest good. —*Cicero*

1640 He is not worthy of the honeycomb that shuns the hive because the bee stings. —*Shakespeare*

1641 The more an idea is developed, the more concise becomes its expression: the more a tree is pruned, the better is the fruit. —*Bougeart*

1642 I can promise to be candid, but I cannot promise to be impartial. —*Goethe*

1643 The cause is hidden, but the result is known. —*Ovid*

1644 Hasten slowly —*Augustus Caesar*

1645 Be slow of tongue and quick of eye. —*Cervantes*

1646 Chance never helps those who do not help themselves. —*Sophocles*

1647 Nothing maintains its bloom forever; age succeeds age. —*Cicero*

1648 The great hope of society is individual character. —*Channing*

1649 Human improvement is from within outward. —*Froude*

1650 Be thou of good cheer. —*Bible*

1651 There's a small choice in rotten apples. —*Shakespeare*

1652 Circumstances! I make circumstances. —*Napoleon*

1653 We can be more clever than one, but not more clever than all. —*La Rochefoucauld*

1654 'Tis always morning somewhere in the world. —*R. H. Horne*

1655 Wind puffs up empty bladders; opinion, fools. —*Socrates*

1656 Character shows itself apart from genius as a special thing. The first point of measurement of any man is that of quality. —*T. W. Higginson*

1657 Everything that happens to us leaves some trace behind; everything contributes imperceptibly to make us what we are. —*Goethe*

1658 It is in men as in soils where sometimes there is a vein of gold which the owner knows not of. —*Swift*

1659 It is part of a prudent man to concilliate the minds of others, and to turn them to his own advantage. —*Cicero*

1660 A man like a watch, is to be valued for his manner of going. —*William Penn*

1661 The integrity of men is to be measured by their conduct, not by their professions. —*Junius*

1662 And let men so conduct themselves in life as to be strangers to defeat. —*Cicero*

1663 Confidence in another man's virtue is no slight evidence of a man's own. —*Montaigne*

1664 Where there is much light the shadow is deep. —*Goethe*

1665 A learned man is a tank; a wise man is a spring. —*W. R. Alger*

1666 Discourse, the sweeter banquet of the mind. —*Homer*

1667 It is good to rub and polish our brain against that of others. —*Montaigne*

1668 Half a man's wisdom goes with his courage. —*Emerson*

1669 And what they dare to dream of, dare to do. —*Lowell*

1670 Nobody's going to make a monkey out of me. —*Clarence Darrow ?*

1671 When desperate ills demand a speedy cure, distrust is cowardice and prudence folly. —*Johnson*

1672 Advise well before you begin; and when you have decided, act promptly. —*Sallust*

OSCAR WILDE
Irish poet and dramatist
October 16, 1854 - November 30, 1900

1673 Take time to deliberate; but when the time for action arrives, stop thinking and go in. —*Andrew Jackson*

1674 It is defeat which educates us. —*Emerson*

1675 Knowledge is the hill which few may hope to climb; duty is the path that all may tread. —*Lewis Morris*

1676 Eloquence is vehement simplicity. —*Burleigh*

1677 Energy and persistence conquer all things. —*Franklin*

1678 Enthusiasm is the fever of reason. —*Victor Hugo*

1679 It is so soon that I am done for, I wonder what I was begun for? —*Epitaph in Cheltenham*

1680 Grace imitates modesty, as politeness imitates kindness. —*Joubert*

1681 Thanks, the exchequer of the poor. —*Shakespeare*

1682 He enjoys much who is thankful for little. A grateful mind is a great mind. —*Secker*

1683 Who's a prince or begger in the grave? —*Otway*

1684 Greatness appeals to the future. —*Emerson*

1685 The greatest man is he who chooses right with the most invincible resolution. —*Seneca*

1686 That man is great who can use the brains of others to carry on his work. —*Donn Piatt*

1687 The lofty oak from a small acorn grows. —*Lewis Duncombe*

1688 True wisdom is the price of happiness. —*Young*

1689 Idleness is the holiday of fools. —*Chesterfield*

1690 The more one endeavors to sound the depths of his ignorance the deeper the chasm appears. —*A. B. Alcott*

1691 Positive in proportion to their ignorance. —*Hosen Ballou*

1692 That man is great who rises to the emergencies of the occasion, and becomes master of the situation. —*Donn Piatt*

1693 Some are born great, some achieve greatness, and some have greatness thrust upon 'em. —*Shakespeare*

1694 He who has imagination without learning has wings but no feet. —*Joubert*

1695 Impossible desires are the height of unreason. —*Haliburton*

1696 Independence, like honor, is a rocky island, without a beach. —*Napoleon*

1697 I would rather sit on a pumpkin, and have it all to myself, than to be crowded on a velvet cushion. —*Thoreau*

1698 The man is best served who has no occasion to put the hands of others at the end of his own arms. —*Rousseau*

1699 We hold these truths to be self-evident: that all men are created equal; that they are endowed by their Creator with certain inalienable rights; that among these are life liberty, and the pursuit of happiness. —*Thomas Jefferson*

1700 Plough deep while sluggards sleep. —*Franklin*

1701 Genius begins great works, labor alone finishes them. —*Joubert*

1702 Diligence is the mother of good luck. —*Franklin*

1703 Shortly his fortune shall be lifted higher; true industry doth kindle honour's fire. —*Shakespeare*

1704 The great end of all human industry is the attainment of happiness. —*Hume*

1705 The finite is annihilated in the presence of infinity, and becomes a simple nothing. —*Pascal*

1706 I am part of all that I have not. —*Tennyson*

1707 A drop of ink may make a million think. —*Byron*

1708 Though this be madness yet there is method in it. —*Shakespeare*

1709 The seeds of first instructions are dropp'd into the deepest furrows. —*Tupper*

1710 The way to procure insults is to submit to them. A man meets with no more respect than he exacts. —*Hazlitt*

1711 Even a hare, the weakest of animals, may insult a dead lion. —*Aesop*

1712 Hell is paved with good intentions. —*Johnson*

1713 Interest blinds some people, and enlightens others. —*La Rochefoucauld*

1714 Nothing of worth or weight can be achieved with half a mind, with a faint heart, and with a lame endeavor. —*Barrow*

1715 A jest loses its point when he who makes it is the first to laugh. —*Schiller*

1716 I wish you all the joy that you can wish. —*Shakespeare*

1717 We lose the peace of years when we hunt after the rapture of moments. —*Bulwer-Lytton*

1718 What is joy? A sunbeam between two clouds. —*Madame Deluzy*

1719 The more one judges the less one loves. —*Balzac*

1720 The king is but a man, as I am, the violet smells to him as it does to me. —*Shakespeare*

1721 Knowledge comes, but wisdom lingers. —*Tennyson*

1722 A Persian philosopher, being asked by what method he had acquired much knowledge, answered, "By not being prevented by shame from asking questions where I was ignorant."

1723 Get the fish, forget the pole. —*Vietnamese proverb*

1724 The journey is hard not because of high mountains and wide rivers, but for fear to meet the challenge. —*Vietnamese proverb.*

1725 When the ox dies, leather remains. —*Vientamese proverb.*

1726 If you have only one dollar left in the world, buy flowers.

1727 All progress has resulted from people who took unpopular positions. —*Adlai Stevenson*

1728 In literature as in love, we are astonished at what is chosen by others. —*Andre Maurois*

1729 Be nice to people on your way up, because you meet 'em on your way down. —*Jimmy Durante*

1730 I hope to have grandchildren, so I can tell them about this experience.

1731 Learning makes a man fit company for himself. —*Young*

1732   Personal liberty is the paramount essential to human dignity and human happiness. —*Bulwer-Lytton*

1733   Every library should try to be complete on something, if it were only the history of pin-heads. —*Holmes*

1734   A great library contains the diary of the human race. —*George Dawson*

1735   Life in itself is neither good nor evil, it is the scene of good or evil, as you make it. —*Montaigne*

1736   Life is a comedy to him who thinks and a tragedy to him who feels. —*Horace Walpole*

1737   Plunge boldly into the thick of life! Each lives it, not to many is it known; and seize it where you will, it is interesting. —*Goethe*

1738   Logic works; metaphysic contemplates. —*Joubert*

1739   The language of woman should be luminous, but not voluminous. —*Douglas Jerrold*

1740   No man can lose what he never had. —*Izaak Walton*

1741   Things unhoped for happen oftener than things we desire. —*Plautus*

1742   Past all shame, so past all truth. —*Shakespeare*

1743   Justice, not the majority, should rule. —*Bouvee*

1744   It never troubles the wolf how many the sheep are. —*Virgil*

1745   Malice blunts the point of wit. —*Douglas Jerrold*

1746   Man is a piece of the universe made alive. —*Emerson*

GEORGE BERNARD SHAW
Irish dramatist
July 26, 1856 - November 2, 1950

1747   Life is a gift to do with what you want.

1748   Man was born for two things — thinking and acting. —*Cicero*

1749   Every man is a volume, if you know how to read him. —*Channing*

1750   Man is an animal that makes bargains; no other animal does this, — one dog does not change a bone with another. —*Adam Smith*

1751   Make yourself an honest man, and then you may be sure that there is one rascal less in the world. —*Carlyle*

1752   The very substance which last week was grazing in the field, waving in the milk pail, or growing in the garden, is now become part of the man. —*Dr Watts*

1753   Let us not forget that man can never get away from himself. —*Goethe*

1754   Nothing so much prevents our being natural as the desire of appearing so. —*La Rochefaucauld*

1755   Maxims are the condensed good sense of nations. —*Sir J. Mackintosh*

1756   Nothing is thoroughly approved but mediocrity. The majority have established this. —*Pascal*

1757   The life of the dead is placed in the memory of the living. —*Cicero*

1758   Mind unemployed is mind unenjoyed. —*Bovee*

1759   Men posessing minds which are morose, solemn, and inflexible, enjoy, in general, a greater share of dignity than of happiness. —*Bacon*

1760   A mere madness, to live like a wretch, and die rich. —*Burton*

1761   Groan under gold, yet weep for want of bread. —*Young*

1762 We have seen better days. —*Shakespeare*

1763 Our greatest misfortunes come to us from ourselves. —*Rousseau*

1764 The greatest misfortune of all is not to be able to bear misfortune. —*Bias*

1765 Mishaps are like knives, that either serve us or cut us, as we grasp them by the blade or the handle. —*Lowell*

1766 To step aside is human. —*Burns*

1767 It is best to rise from life as from a banquet, neither thirsty nor drunken. —*Aristotle*

1768 I had rather have a fool to make me merry than experience to make me sad. —*Shakespeare*

1769 Excellence speaks for itself.

1770 Try to make the world a better place.

1771 All wonder is the effect of novelty upon ignorance. —*Johnson*

1772 With oaths like rivets forced into your brain. —*Cowper*

1773 Diplomacy conquers impatience. —*Lee Aaron Ward*

1774 Each one sees what he carries in his heart. —*Goethe*

1775 Only so much do I know as I have lived. —*Emerson*

1776 Narrowness of mind is often the cause of obstinacy; we do not easily believe beyond what we see. —*La Rochefoucauld*

1777 You can reach stupidity only with a cannon ball. —*H. W. Shaw*

1778 All that is great in man comes through work; and civilization is the product. —*Samuel Smiles*

1779 Wave rolling after wave in torrent rapture. —*Milton*

1780 All's not offence that indiscretion finds. —*Shakespeare*

1781 Orthodoxy on one side of the Pyrennees may be heresy on the other. —*Pascal*

1782 To improve the golden moment of opportunity, and catch the good that is within our reach, is the great art of life. —*Johnson*

1783 Strike while the iron is hot. —*Sir Walter Scott*

1784 Not only strike while the iron is hot, but make it hot by striking. —*Cromwell*

1785 There's a time for all things. —*Shakespeare*

1786 Nothing is too late till the tired heart shall cease to palpitate. —*Longfellow*

1787 Occasions are rare; and those who know how to sieze them are rarer. —*H. W. Shaw*

1788 Objects imperfectly discerned take forms from the hope or fear of the beholder. —*Johnson*

1789 Those who cannot themselves observe can at least acquire the observations of others. —*Beaconsfield*

1790 There is no greater wisdom than well to time the beginning and outsets of things. —*Bacon*

1791 Difficulty adds to result, as the ramming of powder sends the bullet the further. —*George Mac Donald*

1792 A certain amount of opposition is a great help. Kites rise against not with the wind. *—John Neal*

1793 The more powerful the obstacle the more glory we have in overcoming it. *—Moliere*

1794 We acquire the strength we have overcome. *—Emerson*

1795 It is not ease, but effort — not facility, but difficulty, that makes men. *—Sam Smiles*

1796 The effects of opposition are wonderful. There are men who rise refreshed on hearing of a threat; men to whom a crisis which intimidates and paralyzes the majority. *—Emerson*

1797 Albert Einstein when asked what was beyond a finite universe, replied, "Gott only knows."

1798 Until digital . . . I did not realize that for thirty years I have been wearing a circular analog, two-hand numeric readout, chronometer.

1799 Never forget the moral abrogation of words astray. *—Dr. George David*

1800 They who have light in themselves will not revolve as satellites. *—Seneca*

1801 Originality is nothing but judicious imitation. *—Voltaire*

1802 Great things cannot have escaped former observation. *—Dr. Johnson*

1803 Who makes quick use of the moment is a genius of prudence. *—Lavater*

1804 To be a great man it is necessary to turn to account all opportunities. *—La Rochefoucauld*

1805 There is a tide in the affairs of men, which, taken at the flood, leads on to fortune. *—Shakespeare*

1806 Give me a chance says Stupid, and I will show you. Ten to one he has had his chance already, and neglected it. —*Haliburton*

1807 Asked at a press conference why he always talks about auto trade deficits, Lee Iacocca replied, "Whadya want me to talk about? Tomato puree? Rutabagas?"

1808 Nothing is so often irrevocably neglected as an opportunity of daily occurrence. —*Marie Ebner-Eschenbach*

1809 Great men should think of opportunity and not of time. That is the excuse of feeble and puzzled spirits. —*Earl of Beaconsfield*

1810 Be the first to say what is self-evident, and you are immortal. —*Ebner-Eschenbach*

1811 If you would create something, you must be something. —*Goethe*

1812 The little mind who loves itself will write and think with the vulgar; but the great mind will be barely eccentric, and scorn the beaten road. —*Goldsmith*

1813 Excess in apparel is another costly folly. The very trimming of the vain world would clothe all the naked ones. —*William Penn*

1814 Deeds of lowly virtue fade before the glare of lofty ostentation. —*Klopstock*

1815 Do what good thou canst unknown; and be not vain of what ought rather to be felt than seen. —*William Penn*

1816 They used to think they were doing God a favor to print His name in capital letters. —*Richter*

1817 Who is strong? He who subdues his passions. —*Talmud*

1818 Man is only truly great when he acts from passions; never irresistible but when he appeals to the imagination. —*Disraeli*

RUDYARD KIPLING
English author
December 30, 1865 - January 18, 1936

1819 It is not the absence, but the mastery, of our passions, which affords happiness. —*Mme. de Maintenon*

1820 Strong as our passions are, they may be starved into submission, and conquered without being killed. —*Colton*

1821 Study the past if you would derive the future. —*Confucius*

1822 Things without remedy should be without regard; what is done is done. —*Shakespeare*

1823 The present is only intelligible in the light of the past. —*Trench*

1824 Patience is the key of content. —*Mahomet*

1825 What I have done is due to patient thought.. —*Sir Isaac Newton*

1826 To endure is greater than to dare. —*Thackery*

1827 If knowledge is power, patience is powerful. —*Robert Hall*

1828 To bear is to conquer our fate. —*Campbell*

1829 Patience is a necessary ingredient of genius. —*Disraeli*

1830 They also serve who only stand and wait. —*Milton*

1831 Accustom yourself to that which you bear ill, and you will bear it well. —*Seneca*

1832 Originality is the one thing to which unoriginal minds cannot feel the use of. —*John Stuart Mill*

1833 One couldn't carry on life comfortably without a little blindness to the fact that everything has been said better than we can put it ourselves. —*George Eliot*

1834 The noblest motive is the public good. —*Virgil*

1835 The man who loves home best, and loves it most unselfishly, loves his country best. —*J. G. Holland*

1836 I love my country's good, with a respect more tender, more holy and profound than my life. —*Shakespeare*

1837 We hope for a living peace, not a dead one. —*Carlyle*

1838 Deep-versed in books, and shallow in himself. —*Milton*

1839 Opinionated assurance. —*Wendell Phillips*

1840 The most annoying of all blockheads is a well-read fool. —*Bayard Taylor*

1841 Pens carry further than rifled cannon. —*Bayard Taylor*

1842 Patience is the support of weakness; impatience is the ruin of strength. —*Colton*

1843 There is, however, a limit at which forbearance ceases to be a virtue. —*Burke*

1844 By gaining the people, the kingdom is gained; by losing the people, the kingdom is lost. —*Confucius*

1845 The more sand has escaped from the hour-glass of our life, the clearer we should see through it. —*Richter*

1846 Trifles make perfection; but perfection is no trifle. —*Michaelangelo*

1847 The virtue lies in the struggle, not in the prize. —*R. M. Milnes*

1848 Hard pounding, gentlemen; but we will see who can pound the longest. —*Wellington at Waterloo*

1849 By gnawing through a dyke even a rat may drown a nation.
—*Edward Burke*

1850 There is no royal road to anything. One thing at a time, all things in succession. That which grows slowly endures. —*J. G. Holland*

1851 Searching for the best maxims, is like a scavenger hunt of great minds.

1852 There is no creature so contemptible but by resolution may gain his point. —*L'Estrange*

1853 Perseverance and tact are the two great qualities most valuable for all men who would mount, but especially for those who have to step out of the crowd. —*Earl of Beaconsfield*

1854 As said to a head space engineer, a pompous one, on why there was a difference in a spectrophotometer I was demonstrating, "Sir, this unit has reproducible operating parameters with an extensive dynamic range."

1855 The nerve that never relaxes, the eye that never blenches, the thought that never wanders — these are the masters of victory. —*Burke*

1856 Few things are impracticable in themselves; and it is for want of application, rather than of means, that men fail of success.
—*La Roche foucauld*

1857 The block of granite, which was an obstacle in the pathway of the weak, becomes a stepping-stone in the pathway of the strong.
—*Carlyle*

1858 I'm proof against that word "failure." I've seen behind it. The only failure a man ought to fear is failure in cleaving to the purpose he sees to be best. —*George Elliot*

1859 Did you ever hear of a man who had striven all of his life faithfully and singly towards an object, and in no measure obtained it? If a man constantly aspires is he not elevated. —*Thoreau*

1860 Yonder palace was raised by single stones, yet you see its height and spaciousness. He that shall walk with vigor three hours a day will pass in seven years a space equal to the circumference of the globe. —*Johnson*

1861 Life affords no higher pleasure than that of success to another, forming new-wishes and seeing them gratified. —*Dr. Johnson*

1862 It is all very well to tell me that a young man has distinguished himself by a brilliant first speech ... but show me a young man who has not succeeded at first, and nevertheless has gone on, and I will back that young man to do better. —*Charles James Fox*

1863 The quarry becomes a pyramid.

1864 Persuasion tips his tongue whenever he talks. —*Colley Cibber*

1865 Philosophy is the art of living. —*Plutarch*

1866 Create your own business, and then you can't get fired.

1867 All philosophy lies in two words, "sustain" and "abstain."

1868 Kings will be tyrants from policy, when subjects are rebels from principle. —*Burke*

1869 He has mastered all points who has combined the useful with the agreeable. —*Horace*

1870 There is nothing of which nature has been more bountiful than poets. They swarm like the spawn of codfish, with a viscous fecundity that invites and requires destruction. —*Sydney Smith*

1871 It is medecine, not poison, I offer you. —*Lessing*

1872 It is easiest to "be all things to all men," but it is not honest. Self-respect must be sacrificed every hour in the day. —*Lincoln*

1873   Although the last, not least. —*Shakespeare*

1874   As you sow y' are like to reap. —*Butler*

1875   At our wittes end. —*Heywood*

1876   As clear and as manifest as the nose in a man's face. —*Burton*

1877   Build castles in Spain. —*Herbert*

1878   Build castles in the air. —*Burton*

1879   But never the rose without. —*Herrick*

1880   Better late than never. —*Dionysius*

1881   Birds of a feather will gather together. —*Burton*

1882   Better half a loafe than no bread. —*Camden*

1883   Blood is thicker than water. —*Scott*

1884   By hooke or crooke. —*Heywood*

1885   Can one desire too much of a good thing? —*Cervantes*

1886   Dark as pitch. —*Bunyan*

1887   Deeds not words. —*Beaumont and Fletcher*

1888   Every man is the architect of his own fortunes. —*Sallust*

1889   Fortune befriends the bold. —*Cicero*

CHARLES F. KETTERING
American engineer and inventor
August 29, 1876 - November 25, 1958

1890   He knew what is what. —*Skelton*

1891   I have other fish to fry. —*Cervantes*

1892   I am almost frightened out of my seven senses. —*Cervantes*

1893   Ill blows the wind that profits nobody. —*Shakespeare*

1894   Let us do or die. —*Burns*

1895   Leap out of the frying pan into the fire. —*Cervantes*

1896   Life is short, yet sweet. —*Euripides*

1897   More knave than fool. —*Cervantes*

1898   No rule is so general, which admits not some exception. —*Burton*

1899   Nothing is certain but death and taxes. —*Franklin*

1900   Others set carts before the horses. —*Rabelais*

1901   Out of syght, out of mynd. —*Googe*

1902   Smooth runs the water where the brook is deep. —*Shakespeare*

1903   The end must justify the means. —*Prior*

1904   Thoughts rule the world. —*Emerson*

1905   Time is the wisest counsellor. —*Pericles*

1906   Carl Lewis, the multi-gold medal winner of Olympic fame, mentioned that when he tried the decathlon he had the most trouble with the pole vault. Most of us would.

1907 I would if I could, but I can't so I won't.

1908 Defeat is bitter; revenge is sweet.

1909 Television is chewing gum for the eyes.

1910 Hernando Cortes stated at the beginning of his conquest of South America: Great things were never had without exertion. Though we are few in number, we are strong in resolution.

1911 Pretension is nothing; power is everything. —*Whipple*

1912 Concentration is the secret of strength in politics, in war, in trade, in short in all management of human affairs. —*Emerson*

1913 He who is lord of himself, and exists upon his own resources, is a noble but a rare being.

1914 Ideas are something; execution is everything.

1915 First man: I believe everyone should have at least two friends. My only friend is my dog.
Second man: I'll bring you another dog.

1916 Buy from those who go to be executed, as they are not caring how cheap they sell; and sell to those who go to be married, as they are not caring how dear they buy. —*Spanish proverb*

1917 Travel is fatal to prejudice. —*Mark Twain*

1918 Abstract truth is the eye of reason. —*Rousseau*

1919 All that lies betwixt the cradle and the grave is uncertain. —*Seneca*

1920 Humility is the light of the understanding. —*Bunyan*

1921 They understand but little who understand only what can be explained. —*Marie Ebner-Eschenbach*

1922 I like to think I am made of star dust, but everybody treats me like dirt.

1923 Discovery consists of looking at the same thing as everybody else and thinking something different. —*Albert Szent-Gyorgyi, Nobel Prize winner*

1924 The improvement of the understanding is for two ends: first, our own increase in knowledge; secondly, to enable us to deliver and make out that knowledge to others. —*Locke*

1925 It is not astonishing that the love of repose keeps us in continual agitation? —*Stanislaus*

1926 The wretched hasten to hear of their own miseries. —*Seneca*

1927 I believe that man to be wretched whom none can please. —*Martial*

1928 One country, one constitution, one destiny. —*Daniel Webster*

1929 This was the most unkindest cut of all —*Shakespeare*

1930 There is nothing that needs to be said in an unkind manner. —*Hosea Ballou*

1931 Live for something. —*Chalmers*

1932 A cock, having found a pearl, said that a grain of corn would be of more value to him. —*Pierre Leroux*

1933 The synonyme of usury is ruin. —*Dr. Johnson*

1934 Extra interest signifies extra risk. —*Wellington*

1935 Vacillation is the prominent feature of weakness of character.
—*Voltaire*

1936 You beat your pate, and fancy wit will come, knock as you please, there's nobody at home. —*Pope*

1937 He trudged along, unknowing what he sought, and whistled as he went, for want of thought. —*Dryden*

1938 It is the flash which appears the thunder bolt will follow. —*Voltaire*

1939 It is a tempest in a tumbler of water. —*Paul, Grand-Duc de Russie*

1940 Do not begrudge the storm it is God's method of gardening.
—*Dwight Casimere*

1941 Pardon me for quoting myself, but I can't find any better quote.

1942 Nothing serious, we are vertical friends.

1943 No man can answer for his own valor or courage till he has been in danger. —*La Rochefoucauld*

1944 Valor would cease to be a virtue, if there were no injustice.
—*Agesilaus*

1945 He who has resolved to conquer or die is seldom conquered; such noble despair perishes with difficulty. —*Corneille*

1946 The Spartans do not inquire how many the enemy are, but where they are. —*Agis II*

1947 I love the man that is modestly valiant; that stirs not till he most needs, and then to purpose. A continued patience I commend not.
—*Feltham*

1948 The love of glory, the fear of shame, the design of making a fortune, the desire of rendering life easy and agreeable, and the humor of pulling down other people, are often the causes of that valor so celebrated among men. —*La Rochefoucauld*

1949 The soul of this man is in his clothes. —*Shakespeare*

1950 It is our own vanity that makes the vanity of others intolerable to us. —*La Rochefoucauld*

1951 Pride makes us esteem ourselves; vanity makes us desire the esteem of others. —*Blair*

1952 Vice stings us even in our pleasures, but virtue consoles us even in our pains. —*Cowper*

1953 Happy is the man who can endure with equanimity the highest and the lowest fortune. —*Seneca*

1954 Sometimes hath the brightest day a cloud: and, after summer evermore succeeds barren winter, with his wrathful nipping cold: so cares and joys abound, as seasons fleet. —*Shakespeare*

1955 Victory or Westminster Abbey. —*Nelson*

1956 Who overcomes by force, hath overcome but half his foe. —*Milton*

1957 We conquered France, but felt our captive's charms. Her arts victorious triumphed o'er our arms. —*Pope*

1958 Vigilance is not only the price of liberty, but of success of any sort. —*Beecher*

1959 He is most safe from danger, who, even when safe, is on his guard. —*Syrus*

1960 The virtue of man ought to be measured not by his extraordinary exertions, but by his every-day conduct. —*Pascal*

ALBERT EINSTEIN
German-American physicist
March 14, 1879 - April 18, 1955

1961 Fish and visitors smell in three days. —*Franklin*

1962 The bitter clamour of two eager tongues. —*Shakespeare*

1963 Every individual has a place to fill in the world, and is important, in some respect, whether he chooses to be so or not. —*Hawthorne*

1964 He can feel no little wants who is in pursuit of grandure. —*Lavater*

1965 Wealth may be an excellent thing, for it means power, it means leisure, it means liberty. —*Lowell*

1966 Her words but wind, and all her tears but water. —*Spencer*

1967 Cervantes shrewdly advises to lay a bridge of silver for a flying enemy. —*Whipple*

1968 To manage men one ought to have a sharp mind in a velvet sheath. —*George Eliot*

1969 At court one becomes a sort of human ant-eater and learns to catch one's prey by one's tongue. —*Bulwer-Lytton*

1970 Honesty is the best policy, says the familiar axiom; but people who are honest on that principle defraud no one but themselves. —*James A. Garfield*

1971 O, he sits high in all the people's hearts; and that, which would appear offence in us, his countenance, like richest alchymy, will change to virtue and worthiness. —*Shakespeare*

1972 To please the many is to displease the wise. —*Plutarch*

1973 The ladies call him sweet; the stairs, as he treads on them, kiss his feet. —*Shakespeare*

1974 Please not thyself the flattering crowd to hear; 'tis fulsome stuff, to please the itching ear. Survey the soul, not what thou does appear, but what thou art. —*Persius*

1975 Popularity is like the brightness of a falling star, the fleeting splendor of a rainbow, the bubble that is sure to burst by its very inflation. —*Chatfield*

1976 I take sanctuary in an honest mediocrity. —*Bruyere*

1977 Where you are is of no moment, but only what you are doing there. It is not the place that enobles you, but you the place; and this only by doing that which is great and noble. —*Petrarch*

1978 All comes from and will go to others. —*George Herbert*

1979 Our material posessions, like our joys, are enhanced in value by being shared. Hoarded and unimproved property can only afford satisfaction to a miser. —*G. D. Prentice*

1980 When I behold what pleasure is pursuit, what life, what glorious eagerness it is, then mark how full possession falls from this, how fairer seems the blossom than the fruit. —*T. B. Aldrich*

1981 This letter is too long by half a mile. —*Shakespeare*

1982 Good-bye — my paper's out so nearly, I've only room for, Yours sincerely. —*Moore*

1983 The judgement of posterity is truer, because it is free from envy and malevolence. —*Cicero*

1984 My poverty, but not my will, consents. —*Shakespeare*

1985 Through tattered clothes small vices do appear; robes and furred gowns hide all. —*Shakespeare*

1986 What a person praises is perhaps a surer standard, even than what he condemns, of his own character, information and abilities. —*Hare*

1987   Precepts or maxims are of great weight; and a few useful ones at hand do more toward a happy life than whole volumes that we know not where to find. —*Seneca*

1988   The desire of appearing clever often prevents our becoming so. —*La Rochefoucauld*

1989   A snob is that man or woman who is always pretending to be something better — especially richer or more fashionable — than he is. —*Thackery*

1990   Pride eradicates all vices but itself. —*Emerson*

1991   Some people are proud of their humility. —*Beecher*

1992   There is none so homely but loves a looking-glass. —*South*

1993   Pride is increased by ignorance; those assume the most who know the least. —*Gay*

1994   A mind that is conscious of its integrity scorns to say more than it means to perform. —*Burns*

1995   Despatch is the soul of business. —*Lord Chesterfield*

1996   Timely service, like timely gifts, is doubled in value. —*George Mac Donald*

1997   I shall always consider the best guesser the best prophet. —*Cicero*

1998   Arrogance is the outgrowth of prosperity. —*Plautus*

1999   It shows a weak mind not to bear prosperity as well as adversity with moderation. —*Cicero*

2000   Consensus is when we have a discussion. They tell me what they think. Then I decide. —*Lee Iacocca*

ALDOUS HUXLEY
English author
July 26, 1894 - November 22, 1963

2001 Ink is the blood of the printing press. —*Milton*

2002 By the streets of "By and By" one arrives at the house of "Never."
—*Cervantes*

2003 There is a frightful interval between the seed and the timber.
—*Johnson*

2004 We are never present with but always beyond ourselves. Fear, desire,
and hope are still pushing us on towards the future. —*Montaigne*

2005 Nature knows no pause in progress and development, and attaches
her curse on all inaction. —*Goethe*

2006 The infinitely little have a pride infinitely great. —*Voltaire*

2007 Ay, do despise me, I'm the prouder for it; I like to be despised.
—*Brickerstaff*

2008 If he could only see how small a vacancy his death would leave, the
proud man would think less of the place he occupies in his lifetime.
—*Legouve*

2009 If a man has a right to be proud of anything, it is of a good action
done as it ought to be, without any base interest lurking at the
bottom of it. —*Sterne*

2010 What is the meaning of life? Only man can ask, only man can answer.
—*R. T. M.*

2011 More in prosperity is reason tost than ships in storms, their helms and
anchors lost. —*Sir J. Denham*

2012 Proverbs are the wisdom of the wise and the experience of ages.
—*Disraeli*

2013 The proverbs of a nation furnish the index to its spirit, and the results
of its civilization. —*J. G. Holland*

2014 Proverbs are mental gems gathered in the diamond districts of the mind. —*W. R. Alger*

2015 If you hear a wise sentence or an apt phrase, commit it to your memory. —*Sir Henry Sidney*

2016 The study of proverbs may be more instructive and comprehensive than the most elaborate scheme of philosophy. —*Motherwell*

2017 The proverb answers where the sermon fails, as a well-charged pistol will do more execution than a whole barrell of gunpowder idly exploded. —*W. G. Simms*

2018 Short, isolated sentences were the mode in which ancient wisdom delighted to convey its precepts for the regulation of human conduct. —*Warburton*

2019 A carpenter's known for his chips. —*Swift*

2020 A dwarf on a giant's shoulder sees further of the two. —*Herbert*

2021 A happy accident. —*Mme. De Stael*

2022 A little more than kin and less than kind. —*Shakespeare*

2023 All that glisters is not gold. —*Cervantes*

2024 All's well that ends well. —*Shakespeare*

2025 When all is said and done, more will be said than done.

2026 If at first you don't succeed, you're about average.

2027 Where there is light, there are bugs.

2028 When you are up to your neck in crocodiles, it is hard to remember that your original objective was to drain the swamp.

2029 A man makes a decision, and then he makes it right.

2030 Those aren't wrinkles, they're character lines.

2031 Today begins tomorrow.

2032 Your horizon is at the end of your arm, and every step broadens your horizon.

2033 Three people were asked what they would do if all the world were underwater: First; would party to the end. Second; would pray for salvation. Third; would gather together the greatest scientific minds, and learn how to live underwater.

2034 I don't understand why women want to be equal to men. Why should they lower themselves?

2035 When Benny Bufano, the great San Francisco sculptor, was asked how he created his beautiful marble elephant, he replied, "I just chip away everything that doesn't look like an elephant."

2036 Until one is commited, there is hesitancy ... Whatever you can do or dream you can, begin it; boldness has genius, power and magic in it.
—*Goethe*

2037 There are degrees of interest and learning. One wishes to look through the telescope; another inquires how the lens was ground.

2038 Applies to dogs in English parks, but seems appropriate for humans in life: No illegal romping. No fouling of the footpaths.

2039 Go for broke.
—*Motto of the Japanese-American combat team serving in Italy.*

ERIC HOFFER
American author
July 25, 1902 - May 21, 1983

2040 To be a success:
1. Make up your mind what you want to do.
2. Take nothing for granted.
3. Have a plan and work your plan.

2041 It ain't over 'till it's over.—*Casey Stengle*

2042 On the day of victory no one is tired.
—*Arab proverb*

2043 Human beings can alter their lives by altering their attitudes
of mind.—*William James*

2044 Progress always involves risk. You can't steal second base and keep
your foot on first.—*Fredrick Wilcox*

2045 Don't compete. Create. Find out what everyone else is doing and
then don't do it.—*Joel Weldon*

2046 The way to develop decisiveness is to start right where you are, with
the very next question you face.—Napoleon Hill

2047 If Karl instead of writing a lot about capital, made a lot of capital, it
would have been much better. —*Henrietta Marx, Karl's mother*

2048 What is past is prologue —*Shakespeare*

2049 DON'T FORGET!
LOAN AMOUNT = PURCHASE PRICE (—) DOWN PAYMENT
EFFECTIVE GROSS INCOME = GROSS INCOME (—) VACANCY
FACTOR
     & BAD DEBTS
NET INCOME = EFFECTIVE GROSS INCOME (—) EXPENSES
CASH FLOW = NET INCOME (—) DEBT SERVICE
NET SPENDABLE INCOME = CASH FLOW (—) INCOME TAX
     Insert your own numbers & that's it.

2050 Patience after a decision is negligence. —*R. T. M.*

2051 . . . it is good for us to be here. —*Mark 9:5*

2052 The strength of a nation lies in the homes of its people.
—*Abraham Lincoln*

2053 The road to wealth is as plain as the road to the mill.
—*Benjamin Franklin*

2054 No horse has ever won a race it didn't enter.

2055 All a person can do in this life is to gather about him his integrity, his imagination, his individuality — and with these ever with him, out front and in sharp focus, leap into the dance of experience. —*Tom Robbins*

2056 Fifteen billion years ago (round number) all of the real estate in the universe could fit on the head of a pin.

2057 God needed but ten commandments to direct our lives, our federal government needs 7,500 codes just for taxes.

2058 Any man can make paper, only God can make dirt.

2059 Don't sell when the price goes down, "I'm locked in;" don't sell if it goes up, "I can't afford the taxes."

2060 Obstacles are opportunities to develop one's sense of humor.

2061 Beware of self-fulfilling prophesies.

2062 One man's ceiling is another man's floor.

2063 Under all is the land.

ROY OF ROT

MY FAVORITE QUOTES

Number

THE
END

FOR NOW

MAILING LIST

HI, DROPZONE PRESS
PLEASE ADD MY NAME
TO YOUR FLOPPY DISK
FOR FUTURE MAILINGS!

Please print using one square for each letter.

NAME

ADDRESS

CITY

STATE   ZIP

Please fold this envelope as indicated on other side and staple or seal.

ORDER FORM

QUANTITY	ITEM	EACH PRICE	TOTAL
	Roy's Rot *Rules of Thumb to Wit & Wisdom*	12.95	$ _____
	PLAQUE: Dark lettering on gold finish, with 8"x10" walnut plaque. Ready to hang. *Roy's* *First* *Rot #* *Two Words*	19.95	$ _____
	Real Estate Quick & Easy *by Roy T. Maloney*	14.95	$ _____
	TOTAL ORDER		$ _____

☐ I have enclosed my check or money order. I understand each price includes shipping and handling charges.

Please make checks payable to:

R. Maloney, DZ Press

SEND ORDER TO: (Please Print)

NAME _____

ADDRESS _____

CITY _____ STATE _____ ZIP _____

PHONE (Area Code) _____

Please add my friend to your mailing list:

_____

_____

DROPZONE PRESS UNCONDITIONAL GUARANTEE

YOU MUST BE SATISFIED. IF YOU FEEL ANY PRODUCT IS NOT SATISFACTORY, YOU CAN RETURN IT WITHIN 30 DAYS FOR A FULL AND IMMEDIATE REFUND.

Please fold this envelope as indicated on other side and staple or seal.

FROM: _____

_____

_____

_____

DROPZONE PRESS
P. O. Box 882222
San Francisco CA 94188

ORDER FORM

QUANTITY	ITEM	EACH PRICE	TOTAL
	Roy's Rot *Rules of Thumb to Wit & Wisdom*	12.95	$ _____
	PLAQUE: Dark lettering on gold finish, with 8"x10" walnut plaque. Ready to hang. *Roy's First* *Rot # Two Words*	19.95	$ _____
	Real Estate Quick & Easy *by Roy T. Maloney*	14.95	$ _____
	TOTAL ORDER		$ _____

☐ I have enclosed my check or money order. I understand each price includes shipping and handling charges.

Please make checks payable to:

R. Maloney, DZ Press

SEND ORDER TO: (Please Print)

NAME _____

ADDRESS _____

CITY _____ STATE _____ ZIP _____

PHONE (Area Code) _____

Please add my friend to your mailing list:

_____

_____

DROPZONE PRESS UNCONDITIONAL GUARANTEE

YOU MUST BE SATISFIED. IF YOU FEEL ANY PRODUCT IS NOT SATISFACTORY, YOU CAN RETURN IT WITHIN 30 DAYS FOR A FULL AND IMMEDIATE REFUND.

Please fold this envelope as indicated on other side and staple or seal.